Crossway Bible Guide

Series Editors: Ian Coffey (NT), Stephen Gaukroger (OT)
Old Testament Editor: Stephen Dray

Also in this series

Exodus: Stephen Dray
Joshua: Charles Price
Acts: Stephen Gaukroger

Dedicated to my family,
Tina, Wendy, Gareth and Merfyn,
and all the gang in the wider family at the
Anfield Road Fellowship, Liverpool who
have supported and encouraged me in writing
this book, and live by the maxim that as God's people we are
free to build.

Ezra & Nehemiah: Crossway Bible Guide

Free to Build

Dave Cave

Crossway Books
Nottingham

ISBN 1 85684 073-5

Unless otherwise stated, Scripture quotations in this publication are
from the Holy Bible, New International Version. Copyright © 1973,
1978, 1984 International Bible Society. Published in Great Britain by
Hodder & Stoughton Ltd.

Typeset by Anfield Road Fellowship, Liverpool
Printed in Great Britain for Crossway Books, Norton Street,
Nottingham NG7 3HR by Cox & Wyman Ltd, Reading, Berkshire.

Contents

Contents

Illustrations

Maps

Appendix

Crossway Bible Guides

Series Editors' Introduction

Today, the groups of people who meet together to study the Bible appear to be a booming leisure-time activity in many parts of the world. In the United Kingdom alone, over one million people each week meet in home Bible-study groups.

This series has been designed to help such groups and, in particular, those who lead them. We are also aware of the needs of those who preach and teach to larger groups as well as the hard-pressed student, all of whom often look for a commentary that gives a concise summary and lively application of a particular passage. We have tried to keep three clear aims in our sights:

1 To explain and apply the message of the Bible in non-technical language.
2 To encourage discussion, prayer and action on what the Bible teaches.
3 To enlist authors who are in the business of teaching the Bible to others and are doing it well.

All of us engaged in the project believe that the Bible is the Word of God – given to us in order that people might discover Him and His purposes for our lives. We believe that the 66 books which go to make up the Bible, although written by different people, in different places, at different times, through different circumstances, have a single unifying theme: that theme is Salvation.

All of us hope that the books in this series will help people get a grip on the message of the Bible. But most important of all, we pray that the Bible will get a grip on you as a result!

Ian Coffey
Stephen Gaukroger
Series Editors

Note to readers

In our Bible Guides we have developed special symbols to make things easier to follow. Every passage therefore has an opening section which is

the passage in a nutshell

The main section is the one that *makes sense of the passage*.
This is marked with a blackboard.

Questions: Every passage also has special questions for group and personal study in a box after the main section. Some questions are addressed to us as individuals, some speak to us as members of our church or home group, while others concern us as members of God's people worldwide.

Some passages, however, require an extra amount of explanation, and we have put these sections into two categories. The first kind gives additional background material that helps us to understand something complex. For example, if we study the Gospels, it helps us to know who the Pharisees were, so that we can see more easily why they related to Jesus in the way they did. These technical sections are marked with an open book.

Finally, some passages have important doctrines contained in them, which we need to study in more depth if we are to grow as Christians. Special sections that explain them to us in greater detail are marked with a mortar board.

Outlining the issues

With the power struggles of the Assyrian, Babylonian and Persian Empires the Jewish faith had taken a hammering. First the northern kingdom of Israel and then the southern kingdom of Judah had been taken over by invasion armies of the great empires. Many leading families of the tribes of the Hebrew nation had been deported to foreign parts leaving the promised land bereft of effective leadership and the vision, enthusiasm, as well as finance and skills to maintain the holy city of Jerusalem, its Temple and the spirituality of the people.

Certain issues were essential to the survival of the people of God:

Return to the place where God intended his people to be.

Rebuild the Temple of God in order to restore his glory.

Rebuild the urban priority area of Jerusalem and make it a place people would want to live in.

Rebuild the covenant relationship between God and his people through unity of vision, purpose and relationship.

Restore and guard the essentials of faith from compromise on a scriptural basis.

Today an increasing proportion of the peoples of the world live in cities so that, as in the time of Ezra and Nehemiah, the city has become a multinational focus. I believe the call of God to us is to have faith in the city. The same principles of Ezra/Nehemiah's time apply today:

Return to the place where God wants his church to be – for too long we have observed the decline and departure of the church in the big cities of our land.

Rebuild the living Temple – the church – as a place of holiness and a place of prayer so that the name of God will no longer be a curse word on the lips of city dwellers.

Rebuild the urban priority areas – this means Christians getting their hands dirty, dealing with issues from poverty, injustice, homelessness and unemployment to actually improving the physical environment and so halt the decline of the presence and impact of the church in the city.

Rebuild the faith of Christians living in the city who have lost hope, become apathetic and face conditions which have led to the compromising of the essentials of Christian belief.

Restore Christian concern for a biblical basis on which to establish a new morality and vitality which, long term, will not only affect the church but the nation.

The message of Ezra/Nehemiah has not changed – we are still **free to build.**

The time

It is not always easy to appreciate the context of a story unless it can be viewed in a worldwide setting. The accepted time for Nehemiah's arrival in Jerusalem is 445 BC. During 444 BC the wall around Jerusalem was completed, but what was happening in the rest of the world ?

The Great Pyramid of King Cheops in Egypt is already over 2,000 years old.

The Celtic tribes, also known as Gauls or Galatians were dominating central and western Europe and Stonehenge is about 800 years old.

Sixty-two years earlier the Etruscan rulers of Italy lost control of a small city state called Rome when their soldiers were routed just south of Rome by Roman soldiers with some help from the Greeks.

Thirty-nine years previously an Indian nobleman and religious leader called Buddha died.

Kung Fu Tse (Confucius) the Chinese thinker died 35 years earlier.

Greece is on the brink of civil war between the city states of Sparta and Athens. Work on the Parthenon had begun three years earlier.

Socrates the Greek philosopher is 26 years old.

Democrates put forward the theory, in Athens, that all matter is made up of single units called atoms.

Herodotus, from Halicarnassus in Asia Minor, is 40 years old and has just written a book on the wars of Greece against Persia.

Two hundred years later the Maya Indians of Central America would build their first pyramids.

The place

Five hundred years of kings reigning over the Hebrew nation came to a dramatic end in 587 BC when Jerusalem was destroyed and key leaders and people were dragged off into captivity to Babylon.

History shows that this whole area of the Middle East was a place of power struggles between great empires from Egypt to Iran. For a long time the Assyrian Empire had dominated the lands to the south of the Mediterranean Sea. The Jews had rebelled against its rulers on a number of occasions but the northern kingdom of Samaria finally fell to Sargon II of Assyria in 722 BC. Later the Babylonians had beaten the Assyrians and Jerusalem fell to Nebuchadnezzar of Babylon in 597 BC, Solomon's Temple was destroyed ten years later and mass deportations took place. The Babylonians in turn had succumbed to the Persian nation. Then in 538 BC the Persian ruler of the empire granted permission for all exiles who wished it, to return to their home countries.

As we now know, the Jews survived all these events, as well as the empires of the Greeks and the Romans, until they finally returned to their own land over 2,600 years later in the twentieth century.

The books

Ezra and Nehemiah originally formed one book known as the book of Ezra. The first time they are spoken of as two separate books is by someone in the early church called Origen (AD 185–254). It was not until AD 1448 that the division into two books in the Hebrew Bible became completely official.

Who wrote the books and when?

The suggestion is that the author is the same person who wrote the books of Chronicles. That is because the final verses of 2 Chronicles are almost identical with Ezra 1:1–3. Certainly there is a lot of common ground between Chronicles and Ezra/Nehemiah:

Both show a great deal of interest in sacred vessels of the Temple (1 Ch.28:13–19; 2 Ch.5:1 and Ezr.1:7; 7:19; 8:25–30, 33–34). The order of sacrifices and sacrificial materials are almost identical (2 Ch.2:3; 8:13 and Ezr.3:4–6; 1 Ch.29:21; 2 Ch.29:21, 32 and Ezr. 6:9, 17; 7:17–18, 22; 8:35–36).

Liturgical music and instruments, as well as those who are involved are very much the same (1 Ch.15:19; 16:5–6; 25:1, 6; 2 Ch.5:12–13 and Ezr.3:10; Ne.12:35).

The major theme of Chronicles is renewal and reform based on a return to religious faithfulness after years of impurity. The pattern of Ezra/Nehemiah is very similar.

Some say the author is Ezra the scribe. If it is Ezra we know he arrived back in Jerusalem in 458 BC and so he must have written it some time later. It is reasonable to suggest that on this basis it was completed by 400 BC. Whoever wrote it, one thing is clear, they drew upon a number of sources.

Sources for both books are partly based on personal diaries Ezra's diary includes the letter from Artaxerxes (Ezr.7:12–26), Ezra's caravan, a record of those returning to Jerusalem with him (Ezr.8:1–14), and the section on mixing with foreigners (Ezr.10:18–43).

Nehemiah's diary records the building of the wall (Ne.3) and the home-comers (Ne.7:6–73).

Letters in Ezra are written in Aramaic Parts of Ezra are written in Aramaic, the official language of Persian diplomats, rather than Hebrew, the language of the Jews. These sections include the texts of a number of official letters: one to Ahasuerus (4:7) and another to Artaxerxes (4:8), a letter to Darius (5:7–17) and Darius' reply (6:2–12) as well as a copy of a letter by Cyrus (6:2–5).

Registers of names It is obvious that both Ezra and Nehemiah had access to records, most long since lost, which include registers of signatories, names and places (Ezr.2:2–61; 8:2–20; 10:18–43; Ne. 3:1–31; 7:7–63; 10:1–27; 11:4–36; 12:1–26, 32–35, 41–42).

The theme
The dominant theme of both books is restoration or rebuilding: restoration of God's people to the land; restoration of God's glory and honour; his Temple; his city and the covenant between God and the nation of Israel. From a Christian perspective this also sets the scene for the restoration between God and the human race in the coming of Jesus.

Questions which are raised by the books
If Ezra and Nehemiah were in Jerusalem at about the same time why do they seem to ignore each other most of the time (apart from Ne.8:9; 12:36)?

Why did Ezra wait thirteen years to read the Law (Ne.8)?

Ezra returned to a crowded city (Ezr.10:1) but Nehemiah did not (Ne.7:4). In fact he had to encourage people to move into the city.

The high priest when Nehemiah was in Jerusalem was Eliashib (Ne.3:1, 20) but it was Johanan in Ezra's time according to the Elephantine texts from Egypt (see p.21). Johanan is mentioned in Nehemiah 12:11 and verse 22 suggests that he is Eliashib's grandson. But Ezra 10:6 does not refer to Johanan as high priest at all. Nehemiah had to appoint temple treasurers (Ne.11:16; 13:13) but when Ezra arrived they were already there (Ezr.2:43–54).

Ezra thanks God for a wall for Jerusalem (Ezr.9:9) which appears to presuppose Nehemiah's wall, but is it a figure of speech?

Would Nehemiah's reforms be needed if Ezra had done his job properly twenty-five years earlier?

So who came first, Ezra or Nehemiah?

These questions are still being debated, but I have attempted to put my own thoughts forward as the text unfolds.

The date of Ezra and Nehemiah

There are a variety of suggestions for the dating of Ezra and Nehemiah but one thing which is certain is that it could not have been written before 430 BC because some of the events which are recorded did not take place until this date. Ezra is active in 458 BC, and Nehemiah returned to Jerusalem in 445 BC.

Some scholars have argued for a date around 300 BC because they identify Jaddua (Ne.12:10–11) as the one mentioned by Josephus as being around during the time of Alexander the Great. I think this is unlikely – see my comments on the text.

A more popular view in recent times is to date Ezra and Nehemiah at around 400 BC because there is no hint of the Greek invasions of Alexander the Great in the text, nor the rebellion against King Artaxerxes by the Jews and the Phoenicians during the middle of the fourth century BC.

So my own conclusion is that Ezra and Nehemiah were written somewhere between 430 and 400 BC.

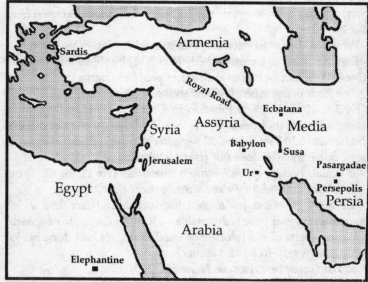

Map 1: The Persian Empire at the time of Ezra and Nehemiah

Chronology

Ezra 1:1-4

God rules OK?

God is in control of his creation and he is God of all the nations not just Israel. He always keeps his promises and, not only is he not limited in his authority but, he can and does speak even to unbelievers.

Here begins the powerful story of a group of people returning to their home country after years of being held against their will in another land. Now it is time to go home and time to rebuild the Temple, as well as God's people. Ezra begins by making it clear to his readers that when God makes a promise, no matter how long it takes, he always keeps his word: then he goes on to make it plain that it is God's Spirit who stirs King Cyrus of the Persians into action.

'The word of the LORD spoken by Jeremiah' (verse 1) refers to the prophecies in Jeremiah 25:11 and 29:10 which promise that the people will be set free after seventy years. Some people think that a week is a long time; seventy years must have seemed an eternity to those waiting on the fulfilment of God's promise through Jeremiah.

What is even more significant is the fact that when Cyrus carried out God's promise and gave the Jews permission to go home the majority decided they did not want to. For years they had prayed for deliverance from captivity and complained that they could not praise God in a foreign land (Ps.137) but now many had done well in business and conflict arose between material comforts and spiritual direction. Only the tribes of Judah and Benjamin, plus a token assortment of priests and Levites, responded to God's call to go home to restore the Temple, the city and the nation (verse 5).

Judah, mentioned in verse three, was the southern half of the land of Israel which split from the north after the death of King Solomon (I Ki.12:20); it included the city of Jerusalem. The tribes occupying this area of Israel were Judah, part of Benjamin which was incorporated into Judah (the other part joining the northern kingdom), and Simeon. It was viewed by biblical writers as the more godly of the two kingdoms because it remained loyal to the house of David, God's chosen king. As the majority of those who returned from Babylon came from Judah the word Jew now came into common use to describe those who came from Israel.

The freewill offering (verse 6) would be an offering made specifically for the rebuilding of the Temple rather than for provisions for the people who were setting off back to Israel. Perhaps it eased the consciences of those who stayed behind in Babylon when they put their hands in their pockets to help those who were actually going to do the work.

Time to go home! The waiting was over and faith is rewarded. Empires may come and go but God keeps his promises to all who put their trust in him; he even puts words into the mouths of kings! The words of Isaiah take on a new freshness: 'Even the youths grow tired and weary, and young men stumble and fall; but those who hope in the LORD will renew their strength' (Is.40:30-31).

The Jews waited nearly 2,000 years after the fall of Jerusalem to the Romans to see the nation of Israel re-established in 1948. How many times must they have questioned Old Testament promises assuring them that God would never forget his people.

They endured persecution over the centuries, from the crusaders from Europe to the Tsars of Russia, Hitler's holocaust to the Arabs. They have suffered the bigotry of literature from Shakespeare's 'Shylock' to Charles Dickens' 'Fagan', but there were always the faithful remnant of the covenant people who were never shaken from the conviction that God was and is always in control and working his purposes out. The message is consistent from the beginning of Ezra to the end of Nehemiah, and is still the same today: God is King of kings and Lord of lords. God rules OK?

Questions

1. *Patience is listed as one of the gifts of the Spirit (Gal.5:22). How would you cope if God told you to wait seventy years before he answered your prayers?*

2. *Which do you think is easiest, to do what God asks you to do, or pay someone else to do it for you? Why?*

3. *How does the Church explain to others that God is in control when, in the short term, evil seems to triumph?*

Personalities

Cyrus of Persia (verse 2) The Cyrus mentioned here is actually Cyrus II, who was the head of a tribe called the Pasargadae from Persia, what is today south Iran. He united the Persians, defeated the Medes (Media is north-west Iran today) and eventually defeated the Babylonians in 539 BC (Babylon is now Iraq).

The Cyrus Cylinder (a clay barrel found in Babylon and now in the British Museum) tells of his victories and his policies with regard to those nations he had captured. It also confirms the opening statement of Ezra that Cyrus gave the Jewish captives permission to go home and rebuild their temple. He died fighting the Massagetai tribes east of the Caspian Sea in the summer of 530 BC and was succeeded by a man called Cambyses.

Biblical terms

The God of heaven (verse 2) is a title used in the Persian period to refer to the God of Israel. Before this time it was one of the titles of the Canaanite god of storms, *Baal-Hadad*. It was not uncommon for a nation to apply titles to their god which were formerly given to the gods of nations they had defeated in battle.

It was used regularly by Jews speaking to foreigners about their God and occurs in this context a number of times in Ezra and Nehemiah (Ezr.1:2; 5:11, 12; 6:9, 10; 7:12, 21, 23; Ne.1:4, 5; 2:4, 20).

It is used frequently in the *Elephantine Papyri* (the name given to a number of 5th century texts which were discovered in AD 1906 at Elephantine island on the river Nile in Egypt regarding life in a Jewish colony there).

Cyrus would also recognize it as a title of the Zoroastrian god *Ahura Mazda*. It was believed he alone was god and created man, darkness and the light (hence the light bulb of that name!).

Ezra 1:5–11

Moved by God

It is important to be both spiritually inspired and practically equipped for God's work.

Sheshbazzar led the return to Israel, restoring the people to the land. Ezra would return later to complete the restoration of the temple.
'Everyone whose heart God had moved' (verse 5) prepared themselves for the task ahead. Money, valuables and livestock were as important as hearts full of enthusiasm for God's call and commission. He had moved the heart of the Persian king so he could move anybody, now the enthusiasm was infectious and everyone was getting involved. The whole people of God have a responsibility and a part to play in assisting the work of the kingdom to progress and now virtually every Jew in Babylon was involved: giving to the cause and helping members of their families who were going back to Jerusalem to prepare for the journey.

The vessels of the Lord's House (verse 9) are not specifically named. What kinds of vessels they were can be discovered by reading 2 Kings 25:14–15. The gold and silver dishes or basins were probably used for pouring out wine (or blood) offerings to God. The number of articles recorded is probably taken from a temple receipt.

Verse 11 mentions 5,400 vessels: the number of items recorded is 2,499 (verses 9–10) but that is probably only a list of the more significant vessels on the inventory. Now they would all be returned to their rightful home in the Temple in Jerusalem under the watchful eye of Sheshbazzar.

Those whose hearts were moved by God responded to the call. The longest journey can often be from the head to the heart. People can sometimes know what God wants from them, but their hearts are not in it. These people had felt the moving of God's Spirit in their hearts and they responded from the heart.

In the New Testament, Cleopas and his friend described how their hearts burned when the resurrected Jesus spoke and shared the Scriptures with them. But it was only in the practical action of breaking bread that they recognized Jesus for who he was (Lk.24:30–32).

When people are moved by God it may begin with the heart but they must also include their time, talents and treasures. Unlike a game of football where twenty-two people put their time as well as energy into the game while thousands sit and stand around the pitch shouting advice, all who are on the Lord's side have a part to play practically as well as spiritually. Real spirituality is always practical when we are moved by God.

Questions

1. How do you react when someone offers you advice on what to do in a particular situation when it is obvious that they have no intention of doing anything practical to help?

2. A number of well known Christians in history have described how a great work of God began in their lives when their hearts were affected. Have you ever felt like that?

3. Paul wrote that God would supply all your needs (Phil.4:19 AV). How does he do that in your church?

Personalities

Nebuchadnezzar (verse 7) Also known as Nebuchadrezzar, he was the ruler over Babylon from 605–562 BC. On 16th March 597 BC his armies laid siege to the city of Jerusalem and having captured its king, Jehoiachin (he only reigned 3 months 10 days) he put Jehoiachin's uncle, Mattaniah-Zedekiah, in charge. An account of this, written in December 597 BC, can be found in a document called The *Babylonian Chronicle* (Tablet Number 21946, the British Museum), and also in 2 Kings 24:10–17. The following April many key people from Judah were taken prisoner back to Babylon (2 Ch.36:10). Ezra 6:5 tells how King Nebuchadnezzar raided the Temple at Jerusalem and took vessels from there back to his own temple, which was dedicated to the Babylonian god Marduk. When he died his son, Amel-Marduk, took the throne.

Sheshbazzar (verse 8) His name is probably derived from a Babylonian root meaning, *May Shammash* (the sun god of the Babylonians – Mithras was the Persian sun god) which means 'protect the father', or *May Sin* (the moon god) 'protect the son'. He was made governor or prince of Judah by Cyrus and was responsible for bringing the temple vessels back to Jerusalem and laying the temple foundations (Ezr.5:14–16). He is mentioned four times in Ezra (1:8, 11; 5:14, 16) and is rather a mystery man as scholars are not even sure whether he was a Jew or a Babylonian. Some people think that this was the Babylonian name for Zerubbabel in the same way as Daniel had a Babylonian name (Dn.1:7) but this seems unlikely. Most scholars now accept that Sheshbazzar and Sheshbazzar of 1 Ch.3:18 are one and the same, which would make him Zerubbabel's uncle.

Ezra 2:1–39

Who's Who?

Know who you are and where your roots are.

The contents of this chapter, with some slight variations, appear also in Nehemiah 7:6–73. The province
mentioned in verse 1 is Judah and not Babylon.

    This list is a 'who's who' of those who returned
from exile. Later generations would look back at it
with great pride if their families and villages were
mentioned. Over 50% of the names on the list are those of families
(verses 2–20) and nearly 30% are the names of villages (verses 21–
35). The remaining names are those of priests (verses 36–39), Levites,
singers, gatekeepers and temple servants (verses 40–58).
   Away from home roots become much more important and, in very
much the same tradition where I grew up in North Wales, people
are described by either their families or the places they came from.
For the Jews, as well as the Irish, the Welsh and the Scots, knowing
where you have come from can be nearly as important as knowing
where you are going to. After all, only the descendant of a priest
could become a priest: it was very much a father-and-son business.
You had to be able to prove your mother was Jewish in order to
establish yourself as Jewish. Hence the dilemma of those listed in
verses 59 and following.
   In any historic list of names there will always be one family name

which looms larger and seems more significant than the rest. This one is no exception and the name 'Parosh' is the largest family listed. Others of the same family are recorded as having returned with Ezra (8:3) and more, bearing the same name, are among those who helped Nehemiah rebuild the walls of Jerusalem (Ne.3:25). Interestingly the name translated means 'Flea', the implication may be that although small it is capable of making its mark on something or someone much larger than itself! David, in a conversation with Saul, implied that he, David, was regarded as a flea (1 Sa.24:14; 26:20). The name probably had more significance then than is now apparent.

The name 'Zerubbabel' (verse 2) probably means 'Seed of Babylon' or 'Born in Babylon', and he was the grandson of Jehoiachin (Ezr.3:2; Hg.1:1; Mt.1:12). He returned with Sheshbazzar, in 537 BC in order to rebuild the Temple and is normally associated with Jeshua. In accounts found in the books of Haggai and Zechariah he was thought by some, for a while, to be messiah, especially as he was a descendant of David (1 Ch.3:19). But Ezra does not seem to share that view as he makes no mention of it.

Jeshua (verse 2) is an Aramaic version of Joshua; he was descended from the last chief priest, Jozadak (1 Ch.6:15), and was probably made high priest at Jerusalem as a result (Zc.3:1). Incidentally, in Aramaic (see note on Ezr.4:7) the name for Jeshua is Jesus, and Jesus would have been known as Jeshua by his family.

Questions

1. Where did your family live three generations ago? Why is it important to know our family background?

2. Do you think that there should be ethnic churches (Welsh, Irish or African for example) or should there be one international church for everybody?

3. How would you demonstrate your relationship to Jesus?

Biblical terms

The Captivity (verse 1) is normally used as a technical term to describe the period of time that the tribes of Israel were forcibly restrained from going back home.

In 722 BC the northern kingdom of Israel was overrun by the Assyrian army and its king, Sargon II, and all but the poor were taken away from their homeland and resettled in Mesopotamia (2 Ki.17:6). Later under a new king, Sennacherib, the Assyrians captured sixty–six cities from the southern kingdom of Judah in 701 BC. (This is according to an account found in palace records excavated at Nineveh some of which is found on the *Taylor Prism*, in the British Museum.)

Then in 598 BC, after the Babylonians had defeated the Assyrians and taken over their empire, Jerusalem was captured and most of its leading citizens also taken to Babylon. By 586 BC the southern kingdom was finished and the Temple destroyed (2 Ki.25:12).

Not much is known about what happened to the exiles over the next sixty years after the fall of Jerusalem, except that King Jehoiachin was released when Evil-Merodach became king of Babylon in 561 BC (2 Ki.25:27–30; he is also mentioned in Babylonian records[1]).

Finally in 538 BC after the Persians had defeated the Babylonians, King Cyrus gave permission for the Jews to return home to their own land, but only a few would return; the rest stayed to become part of what would be known as the *Diaspora* (the Jews of the dispersion).

Personnel

Priests (verse 36) Priests in Israel were the descendants of Aaron, Moses' brother (Nu.10:8). The only word used for priests of the Lord in Hebrew is *Cohen,* although the word is also often used for priests of other gods. Unlike priesthood in the church it was not a vocation but an office: kings were called or chosen by God but not priests. The word which is translated here as 'appoint' or 'consecrate', (for example Ex.28:41) refers to the making of priests, and literally means 'to fill the hand'. It probably originates in the fact that Moses put parts of sacrifices into the hands of Aaron and his sons (Ex.29:24–25; Lv.8:27–28).

They were not ordained as such but they were set apart for God's service and so could set foot on holy ground and handle sacred objects without causing them to become unclean. In order to carry out these tasks priests were forbidden to do certain things.

For instance they could not attend funerals, except for those of close family (Lv.21:1–6). Priests were not allowed to marry prostitutes or divorcees (Lv.21:7) and had to put on special clothes to enter God's sanctuary, as well as wash their clothes (Ex.28:43) and abstain from alcohol (Lv.10:8–11).

Fig. 1: The dress of the High Priest

Ezra 2:40–58

The house of the LORD

Every one of God's people has a part to play in the house of the Lord.

The 'big name' families, as is often the case, are listed first, then the priests. The list continues now with the names of the families of Levites, singers, gate-keepers and Temple servants. In an ever constant concern to cover every detail a note is made of every single task necessary to ensure the house of the Lord could function effectively. It would take all the families and their particular skills to allow the Temple to function as God intended, excluding those who were unable to show they were truly God's people.

In times past, during the monarchy, the Temple had fallen into disrepair on a number of occasions because not everyone had carried out their responsibilities. King Joash had to repair the Temple (2 Ch.24:4) and King Hezekiah actually had to have the doors re-opened and order the Levites to clean out the Temple: rather as a mother orders a child who has not cleaned its room for a long time (2 Ch.29:3–36). In the eighteenth year of King Josiah's reign, it was again necessary to purify the house of the Lord (2 Ch.34:8). This time things had grown so out of hand that the temple staff had managed to lose the Book of the Law, God's written word, and it was only rediscovered during the spring cleaning (2 Ch.34:14).

With this backcloth you can appreciate why it was important to ensure everything was done decently and in order. Churches today suffer the same problems, shabby buildings and surroundings because Christians have opted out of their responsibilities. The issue also arises in the Temple (the gathered congregation of Christians) when believers do not give attention to their duties and responsibilities. The apostle Paul wrote to admonish the church at Corinth because they were gossiping, arguing with each other, taking one another to court and there was even sexual immorality. He said, 'Don't you know that you yourselves are God's temple and that God's Spirit lives in you?' (1 Cor.3:16).

Every believer is a part of the house of the Lord with a duty and responsibility to play his or her part properly.

Questions

1. Do you recognize the responsibilities God has placed on you personally? What are they?

2. In the church you attend, what are the areas of need in order to maintain an effective Christian witness?

3. In the worldwide church would you say God's house is in order?

Personnel

Levites (verse 40) The sons of Levi were set apart (during the Exodus) in order to perform certain sacred functions, such as looking after the Tabernacle or Tent of Meeting (Nu.1:50), and they also had the responsibility of helping Aaron and his descendants in their priestly role (1 Ch.6:48–49). They did not inherit land as the other tribes did (Dt.10:8–9) but they were given an income, towns and pasture-lands amongst the other tribes in which they and their families could live (Nu.35:1–8).

One clan within the tribe of Levi was promised inherited priest-hood, Aaron's family (Ex.29:9, 44; 40:15; Nu.3:4), while the rest of the tribe performed the less important functions: although it must be said that during the time of the Judges, and up to the time of David, not all priests were from the tribe of Levi (Jdg.17:5; 2 Sa.20:26) and the great leader Samuel came from the tribe of Ephraim (1 Sa.1:1). Jeroboam I also appointed non-Levitical priests but was not approved of for having done so (1 Ki.12:31f). Even during this time it was considered preferable to have a priest from the tribe of Levi.

The fact that Levites were considered less important than priests may have had something to do with the reluctance of many of them to return to Israel after the Exile (Ezr.8:15–29).

The Singers (verse 41) The word 'singer' would be more easily translated 'musician' as it can mean those who compose as well as those who perform music. Asaph was made lead singer by King David (1 Ch.16:4–5) and his descendants from then on were mainly used as singers and cymbal players.

The Gatekeepers (verse 42) The gatekeeper's job was to be 'a bouncer', guarding the ritual purity of the Temple area and making sure that the wrong sort of people did not get in (2 Ch.23:19). Some of them looked after the storehouse and treasury in the Temple (1 Ch.9:26–27).

Temple Servants (verse 43) The word 'servants' used here liter-ally means 'the given'. They were regarded as some of the least important of the Temple staff and it was their job to help the Levites (Ezr.8:20).

The names of the Temple servants listed here suggest that most, if not all, were not of Jewish origin. They may well be the group Ezekiel was talking about when he accused Israel of allowing uncircumcised foreigners into the Temple. In verses 43–53 there are Egyptian (Ziha), Syrian (Rezin), Babylonian (Besai), Arabian (Meunim and Nephussim), Edomite (Barkos) and Illyrian (Sisera) names included.

Sons of Solomon's servants (verse 55) The word 'servants' is actually the Hebrew for slaves. Slaves were obtained in a number of ways in Old Testament times, for example: through capture in times of war (Gn.14:21), through purchase (Gn.17:12–13, 27); through failure to pay debts and fines (Ex.22:3; 2 Ki.4:1; Ne.5:5, 8); through kidnap, as Joseph was by his brothers (Gn.37:27–28).

Finally, people could sell themselves or members of their families into slavery to escape poverty, in the knowledge that they would be set free eventually under the requirements of the law of Jubilee (Lv.25:39–43).

Ezra 2:59–63

Missing links

If you are not sure where you fit in – find out.

Everybody wants to feel they are accepted and belong. Those families which Ezra lists in verse 59 would be no exception. They could not be involved in the Temple and share in the portion of food for the priests (Lv.2:3) unless they could fill in the gaps in their family trees.

 Three priestly families and three non-priestly families could not prove they were of good Jewish stock. It may have been that they had lost their family records, although it seems unusual that no one would remember at least some of their ancestors, especially as genealogies were considered important to the Jews. What was more likely was that they had intermarried in Babylon with people from other nations. This could make it impossible to show an unbroken line of Jewish descent. As a result they were regarded as unclean so those who came from the priestly families were not allowed to function as such. They were not permitted to eat the sacred food until the will of God had been sought by the use of the Urim and Thummim by the priest. The order came straight from the top, the governor himself issued it (verse 63). It was a strong incentive to find the missing connections in order to fit into the family and the purposes of God. God would have the final say.

Jesus' family tree (Mt.1) would have raised one or two eyebrows at the time of Ezra. Four women are mentioned in it and three of the four were not of Jewish origin: Rahab (verse 5) was a Canaanite and a prostitute in Jericho (Jos.2:1); Ruth, David's grandmother (verse 5) was a Moabite (Ru.1:4); Uriah's wife, Bathsheba (verse 6) was a Hittite, or at least married to one (2 Sa.11:3).

The importance of belonging to the church 'family' is equally important today and it normally requires some rite acknowledging membership of the family of God: membership, baptism or confirmation. Most church traditions today operate a system of safeguards for sharing bread and wine and some churches will only allow members of their own particular denomination to participate.

The missing connection for those outside the church today is Jesus Christ: he is the missing link who can bring us back into a right relationship with the heavenly Father. The challenge is still the same today: if you are not sure where you fit in, find out.

Questions

1. What do you think is the minimum requirement needed to be called a Christian?

2. What proof should Christians look for in order to relate to other Christians?

3. Who should decide who is acceptable and who is not in the Church?

Personnel

Governor (verse 63) is translated *Tirshatha* in some translations. It is actually a title applied to the governor of Judea, probably Sheshbazzar; it is of Persian origin and can most easily be translated *'excellency'*.

Temple worship

Urim and Thummim (verse 63) No one knows for certain exactly what they were or what the words actually mean. What we do know from Bible references was that they were kept in the breastplate, or ephod, of the garments of the high priest (Ex.28:6–30) and were used to discern God's will in times of uncertainty (Nu.27:21; 1 Sa.14:41–42; 23:9–12).

Three answers could be achieved by consulting Urim and Thummim, also known as the sacred lots: yes, no, or neither (rather like heads and tails in the tossing of coins). They were entrusted to the tribe of Levi (Dt.33:8). After the time of King David there is little evidence that they were used and people took to asking prophets or seers to discern the will of God for them. The only other mention is in this verse and Nehemiah 7:65 which suggest that there was no priest who could use them. Nehemiah 10:34 mentions the 'casting of lots' by the priests.

It is thought that they may have been two flat stones, sticks or dice with one side white, the other black; so that, when thrown, if they landed both sides black the answer was 'no', both sides showing white the answer was 'yes' and one displaying white and the other black would mean there was no specific answer.

Ezra 2:64–70

Everything but the kitchen sink

It is important in responding to God's call not to forget the practical requirements.

These few verses include an inventory of people and property. The total of 42,360 people (verse 64) is more than the total obtained by adding together the men of Israel (24,144; verses 2–35); the priests (4,289; verses 36–39); the Levites, singers and servants (733; verses 40–58) and those of unknown families (652; verse 60), where the total comes to 29,818. The gap is probably bridged by adding on women and children who are not mentioned.

Horses, mules, camels and donkeys are on the list but not sheep, goats and cattle. It has been argued that they were not a part of this great caravan because they would have slowed it down significantly. The collection for rebuilding the Temple was substantial. One drachma, if it was a Persian daric, was equivalent to one month's wages for a soldier.

It seems that everything which was vital for the task of rebuilding the Temple was included: the various ministries from priests to musicians; lay people, servants and slaves; horses for military work, mules for the powerful and wealthy, camels to transport heavy loads and donkeys to carry women, children and other loads. They had everything, in fact, except the kitchen sink!

Finance was also a practical consideration if the Temple was to be rebuilt. It was not raised by jumble sales, street-by-street collection, or appeals. It was direct giving by the leaders of the families. They could have argued that the money was needed for them to resettle in and around Jerusalem (verse 70), but they didn't. Real giving, sacrificial giving, came from the conviction that the Lord had need of it. This was a practical demonstration of their faith as well as a witness to the surrounding nations. When they arrived in Jerusalem the people proved their conviction by their giving (verse 68).

An old hymn reflects the kitchen-sink approach: 'Take my life and let it be, consecrated, Lord to thee...take my silver and my gold, not a mite would I withhold'. Each verse builds up the inventory which says 'Use me and everything I have – including the kitchen sink!'

Questions

1. What method do you use in deciding what to give to God's work?

2. How does your Church raise money to carry out the work of the Kingdom of God?

3. Is there anything you would not give up for God?

Coins of the realm

Drachmas (verse 19) The use of coins began in Asia Minor (Turkey today) in the 7th century BC and spread through the influence of the Persian Empire. The gold drachma was possibly intended to mean the Persian daric, introduced by Darius I (see Ezr.4:5; Ne.7:71) and named after him. It weighed 130 grammes. Or it could have been the gold Greek drachma, of which very few were actually in wide circulation. It was only introduced during the reign of Darius I which began in 522 BC. As the date of the Israelites' return (537 BC) was a few years earlier, it has been suggested that the value was put into terms which would be understood at the time of writing rather than the time of the event.

Minas (verse 64) Fifty shekels made a mina or maneh and sixty minas made a talent. They are mentioned frequently in ancient Near Eastern texts (for shekels see note to Ne.5:15).

Fig. 2: A Persian and a Median noble
(from the Great Staircase at Persepolis)

Ezra 3:1–7

Tabernacles and trumpets

The priority of God's people is to give him first place in their lives.

The return of the first group of people was complete: now it was time to re-establish Temple worship in Jerusalem. In the seventh month – the people gathered 'as one man' (verse 1) a phrase which would not be used again until Nehemiah 8. The Hebrew word for the phrase translated into English as 'burnt offerings' (verse 2) is interesting. There is no Hebrew word specifically meaning 'sacrifice', but the nearest is the word *Korban* meaning 'that which is brought near'. One word which is used, *Ola,* is translated as 'burnt offering', and literally means 'that which goes up'. The ritual sacrifice of an animal (or sometimes a person) to a particular deity was common among the nations in Old Testament times. Leviticus 1:3–17, which covers the requirements for burnt offerings, suggests that burnt offerings were made to obtain forgiveness or atonement (Lv.1:4) and that the result is a pleasing smell to God (Lv.1:9, 13, 17).

The Feast of Tabernacles (verse 4) was usually celebrated on the 15th day of the month of Tishri (Ex.23:16; 34:22). It lasted a week and marked the end of the gathering in of grapes. To do this many folk went out in the fields and lived in tents in order to gather in the harvest and so the occasion was used as a reminder of the time when the Jewish people at the Exodus in the time of Moses, lived in tents for forty years. The word 'tabernacle' means 'tent of meeting' and was used to describe the mobile place of worship where the ark of the covenant was kept during the wilderness period of the nation's history; it also has the meaning 'temporary shelters'.

The foundation of the Temple had yet to be laid (verse 6) but that did not stop the Israelites from celebrating in times of worship and sacrifice in complete unity. They didn't make excuses but gave God first place.

When Moses led the people out of Egypt they complained about everything. Nothing to eat, nothing to drink (Ex.15:24; 16:3; 17:3) and they even made another god for themselves (Ex.32:1–10) but today there was no complaining or excuses.

People since have found a variety of reasons (excuses?) for not giving God first place. Some folk came to follow Jesus but had a variety of excuses for putting off a response (Lk.9:57–62). I wonder what would have happened if the believers gathered in the upper room at Pentecost (Acts 2) had decided to get everything right first before they went out to proclaim the Good News? Maybe they would first have had to find a building to meet in, raised the money for the mission, decided on an agreed theology, or waited for a qualified leader – but they didn't. God was given first place and everything else followed. Jesus simply said 'Seek first his kingdom and his righteousness, and all these things will be given to you as well' (Mt.6:33).

There is an old saying which goes, 'If you wait for perfect conditions to sow the seed you will never reap the harvest'. The people of the Return got on with God's work 'despite their fear of the peoples around them' (verse 3). Whatever the cost nothing is achieved by putting off doing God's will, the priority of God's people should be always to give him first place.

Questions

1. *What excuses have you used for putting off God's will in your life?*

2. *If you wait for everything to be perfect before you do anything, how long will you have to wait?*

3. *Is there such a thing as the perfect church on earth? What is there?*

Times and seasons

The seventh month is the month of *Tishri* or *Ethanim* (verse 1) and means 'flowing rivers'. It is equivalent to our September/October. The Jewish calendar is based on the phases of the moon and so each month lasts 28 days. When the calendar becomes a month out the extra month of *Adar Adar* is added, and the month always begins with the new moon.

Geography

Sidon (verse 7) Sidon (modern-day Saida) was a Phoenician port on the coast of Lebanon and a centre of commerce and industry at the time of Ezra.

Tyre (verse 7) The city of Tyre (today's Sûr) was the main port of the Phoenicians and was about 40 kms south of Sidon in Lebanon. It had two harbours, one on the mainland and one on an island opposite.

King Hiram I, a friend of King David, who supplied building materials for the first Temple (2 Sam.5:11; 1 Ki.5:1) and Hiram, a craftsman who helped Solomon build his Temple, both came from here (1 Ki.7:13–14).

The people of Tyre were well known as traders and merchants, as well as slave traders (Joel 3:5–6). Jesus visited the area near to Tyre (Mt.15:21–28), and the people of Tyre listened to him speak (Mk.3:8; Lk.6:17).

Lebanon (verse 7) Lebanon was a mountain range in Syria famous for its trade in timber. The southern end was a continuation of the hills of Galilee. It was 160 kms long and covered with thick forests of myrtles, conifers, and cedars. It is often quoted in the Old Testament as a place of plenty (for example: Ps.72:16; Ho.14:5–7).

The cedars of Lebanon were seen as symbols of power and might (Jdg.9:15; 1 Ki.4:33; 2 Ki.14:9; Is.35:2; 60:13) and they were used for building the great temples and palaces of the surrounding nations, including Israel (1 Ki.5:6, 9, 14).

Joppa (verse 7) Joppa is the old name for the present-day port of Jaffa which extends to Tel Aviv in Israel. It was the nearest natural harbour to Jerusalem, some 55 kms inland, and so was the obvious place to ship materials for the building of the Temple. It was the port that Jonah took a ship from to escape God's will for him, (Jon.1:3) and Peter stayed at Simon the tanner's house in Joppa (Acts 10:32).

Ezra 3:8–13

A firm foundation

Make sure the foundation for your faith is right.

The second month of the Jewish calendar was called *Iyyar* and is equivalent to our April/May. It is interesting to note that Zerubbabel and Jeshua chose this particular time to lay the Temple foundation (verse 8). Solomon chose the same time to carry out the same task with the first Temple (1 Ki.6:1).

The age limit of serving as a Levite had originally been twenty-five years and over (Nu.8:24). Now it has been lowered to twenty years of age (verse 8). The age limit seems to have been reduced at the time of the building of Solomon's Temple (1 Ch.23:24–27). So it appears that they were following the same pattern as Solomon in order to ensure the foundations were properly laid.

The physical task of laying the foundations was followed by a time of celebration 'as prescribed by David' (verse 10) which included thanksgiving and praise (verse 11). The word used here for joy (verses 12 and 13 and in Ezr.6:16, 22; Ne.8:10,12,17; and 12:43), suggests a smiling face and means 'excitement' or 'gladness'. It is viewed not just from the point of view of the individual but the community as well. It is seen as a quality, as well as an emotion, and is frequently linked to the national and religious life experiences of Israel (Ne.8:10f). It is seen in the Old Testament as a mark of the Golden Age (Is.49:13) and in the New Testament is listed as one of the main fruits of the Holy Spirit (Gal.5:22).

A firm foundation was laid because they had followed the instructions laid out in God's word: they laid a firm foundation not only for the building but also in their hearts. They had laid a foundation for their faith in obeying God's instructions.

Later, as we shall see, they began to compromise and water down God's word for them and things changed as a result, but at least the Temple would be built on a firm foundation.

If I buy a piece of furniture from a 'Do It Yourself' shop and ignore the maker's instructions it should come as no surprise if things do not fit together properly. The same is true of the Christian life: for a firm foundation follow the Maker's instructions.

Questions

1. *Do you ever take short cuts in the Christian life? If so, what is usually the result?*

2. *What do you think happens when a church ignores God's instructions?*

3. *How can you build a firm foundation for your faith?*

Temple worship

Vestments (verse 10) During religious celebrations the priests would wear special vestments – normally a linen garment worn around the waist and sometimes called a linen ephod (1 Sa.2:18); it was almost certainly a loin cloth or apron.

The high priest wore a tunic of blue. Over it he wore the robe of the ephod decorated with pomegranates and bells and over this he wore an ephod made of gold. Finally, over all the vestments he wore the embroidered breastplate. This was the jewel-covered pouch carrying the sacred lots Urim and Thummim (see the note on 2:63 and Fig.1). He also wore a white cloak and a special turban (Ex.28; 29:5–6). The Hebrew word for turban meant 'sign of consecration'. Incidentally, the word 'vestry' originally meant 'the wardrobe where the priest's vestments were kept'.

Trumpets (verse 10) Trumpets were used for signalling, calling God's people to assemble together, and to accompany worship (Nu.10:1–10). Priests sounded trumpets in the call to war (2 Ch.13:12–15) and the Jews had a day for blowing trumpets called the 'Feast of Trumpets' in the month of Tishri (Nu.29:1) They were usually made of silver or bronze.

Cymbals (verse 10) Cymbals made of copper were banged together in the Temple to denote beginnings, pauses and endings of chapters of psalms being sung (1 Ch.15:19).

Fig. 3: Temple musician

Ezra 4:1–5

Bribery and corruption

Whenever God calls people to carry out his work the enemy will always be there to try and undermine God's authority.

As soon as work on the Temple began in earnest the enemies of those who had returned moved in. Their strategy in attempting to foil the efforts of Israel in rebuilding the Temple is interesting.

They began with an attempt at infiltration: 'Let us help you build' (verse 2) by suggesting that they shared with Israel common ground in their faiths. At first it seems a reasonable request, until you understand the background.

After the fall of Samaria, the Assyrian invaders followed a familiar pattern of the times by taking away the leading families and replacing them with similar people from other nations. However, when the Babylonians took leading families into exile from the lands of Judah and Benjamin, and the city of Jerusalem they did not replace them. This resulted in the former northern kingdom of Israel developing a mixed religion involving other religions so their tradition was no longer regarded as pure: whereas the former southern kingdom remained loyal to *Yahweh* (the name for God; see the comment on Ezra 4:10).

Following the model of a right foundation, there could be no compromise. The saying 'Cleanliness is next to godliness' took on a much stronger implication here. The rebuke by Zerubbabel, Jeshua and the leaders is carefully worded. 'You have no part ... we alone ... for the LORD [Yahweh], the God of Israel, as King Cyrus ... commanded us' (verse 3). They named the authority of the king and God in dismissing their enemies, appealing to both civil and religious authority.

'The peoples around them' (verse 4) or more literally 'the people of the land' and interchangeable with 'peoples' (Ezr.3:3), refers to the inhabitants of Judah, Samaria, Idumea and other neighbouring regions who are not authentic Jews and by definition, therefore, religiously suspect (see also Ezr.9:1–2, 11; 10:2, 11; Ne.9:24, 30; 10:30–31).

Having failed to dilute things from the inside, the people around them set about attempting to discourage them from the outside. The word 'discourage' (verse 4) in Hebrew literally means 'to weaken the hands' so they would not be able to carry out the work (compare 6:22, and Ne.6:4). Fear is often a good weapon: it had worked very well for Gideon's 300 men fighting against thousands (Jdg.7:16–25); now Israel's enemies were trying the same technique against them, but to little effect.

Finally the opposition hired counsellors to try and intimidate the Jews (verse 5): a method similar to that used later to intimidate Nehemiah (Ne.6:11–13).

Corruption and bribery failed because Israel was convinced that not only the king, but the King of kings was on their side. I wonder if Paul had a situation like this in mind when he wrote, 'if God is for us, who can be against us?' (Rom.8:31).

Questions

1. *If someone of another faith asked to help in your church, what would you do?*

2. *What makes you afraid and how do you deal with that fear?*

3. *How can we demonstrate God's authority as Christians?*

Personalities

Esarhaddon of Assyria (verse 2) He was king of
Assyria 681–669 BC after his father Sennacherib who
was murdered. There is a stele or stone slab known
as the *Stele of Esarhaddon* (British Museum) which
tells of his military exploits and mentions Tyre, Sidon
and Manasseh, king of Judah (2 Ch.33:11).
Esarhaddon is mentioned also in 2 Kings 19:37.

Darius of Persia (verse 5) This is Darius I, ruler of the Persian
Empire (522–486 BC) and not to be confused with Darius the Mede
mentioned in the book of Daniel (Dn.6:6,9, 25). The name means 'he
who sustains good thought'. He became king after the death of
Cambyses, but not before two others tried to take the throne first.
He was the one who allowed the Jews who had returned to build
the Temple in accordance with the statement made by Cyrus.
(Hg.1:1; Zc.1:1) He was also instrumental in the building of the first
version of the Suez canal in Egypt.

Ezra 4:6–24

Take a letter

There have always been those who are ready to spread scandal about God's people in order to try and destroy their credibility.

Someone once said 'the pen is mightier than the sword', and Israel's enemies were out to prove it. They wrote a letter to the authorities accusing the Jews of rebellion (verse 6). The word used for accusation, *Sitna*, is close to the word, 'Satan'. At this period Aramaic (verse 7) was the common language of the Persian Empire: all of Ezra 4:8 – 6:18 is written in Aramaic, as is Ezra 7:12–26. It is quite close to Hebrew in structure and was originally the language of another semitic people, the Aramaeans. Jacob (Dt.26:5) referred to himself as an Aramaean which suggests quite close links. Aram is the biblical name for Syria.

The Persian Empire made use of many people to keep the king informed of any possible threat to his authority (see the note on *satraps* in Ezr.8:36). In Jerusalem it appears Bishlan, Mithsedath, Tabeel (verse 7), Rehum and Shimshai (verse 8) were used. They wrote accusing Israel of restoring Jerusalem in order to plot against the king. They include themselves as deportees living in and around Samaria (verse 10) which was the capital city of the northern kingdom of Israel from the time of King Omri (1 Ki.16:24). It was destroyed by the Assyrians in 721 BC and around 27,000 of its leading citizens were taken off into captivity to Assyria (2 Ki.17:24) and replaced by peoples from other nations who had likewise been captured.

Things did not go well for the newcomers and they believed it was because they were not worshipping the local deity, so one of the Jewish priests in exile was sent back to sort things out. They set up a place of worship at Bethel and a mixed faith developed, partly based on the God of Israel and partly on that of the gods of the foreigners now inhabiting Samaria (2 Ki.17:25–34). As a result, the Jews returning from exile refused to allow these people to have anything to do with the rebuilding of the Temple. They were now regarded as impure. Later some of the Samaritans would set up their own place of worship at Shechem centred on Mount Gerizim (Dt.11:29; Jos.8:33): it was one of their descendants, the Samaritan woman, who questioned Jesus about this (Jn.4:19–20).

Trans-Euphrates (verse 10) or 'the province beyond the river' are the words used in Hebrew to refer to the Persian province west of the Euphrates river, often just referred to as 'the river' in the Old Testament: it included Palestine and Syria.

It was then that another favourite strategy of the dissatisfied came into operation. If the rebuilding were to be allowed, 'no more taxes, tribute or duty will be paid and the royal revenues will suffer' (verse 13). Not only were they trying to undermine Israel, now they were directly challenging the authority of the king. The same situation occurs nowadays: big businesses who do not like Christian influence on the law of the land attack government where it feels most pain, in its purse!

Tax was a fixed annual tribute paid by the province, tribute was a kind of poll tax, and duty was due to a feudal lord (it could be called protection money) and accounted for much individual taxation. It has been estimated that in total Persia took from the Jews, Samaritans and Gentiles of Palestine something in the region of 350 silver talents every year[2]. A talent was equivalent to about 300 people's wages for one year!

Now it was the king's turn to write a letter. A search had been made in the library and a record of a history of revolt was found (verses 18–20; see 2 Ki.18:7; 24:1) and so the order was given for work on the Temple to cease (verse 21). The Jews were compelled by force to stop work (verse 23) and they had no choice but to obey. In the short term scandal had undermined credibility, but not for too long: 'until the second year of the reign of Darius, King of Persia' (verse 24).

The second year of the reign of Darius began on the first day of *Nisan* 520 BC which is estimated as 3rd April; work on the Temple began on 21st September[3]. When the work was stopped the Persian Empire was under threat from a variety of rebels, only when things were stable would the task of rebuilding be permitted to continue, but it would continue.

The history of the church follows a similar pattern. The people carrying out God's work have been persistently persecuted; for example, John Wesley was maligned, often stoned and beaten up for preaching the Good News but he persisted in proclaiming God's kingdom. The early founders of the Pentecostal movement, just after the turn of the twentieth century, were treated in the same way but through persistence have established their credibility in the Christian world.

The Church has been maligned, persecuted, and prevented from carrying out its work by empires from Rome to Russia but still the words of Jesus ring true, 'On this rock I will build my church, and the gates of Hades will not overcome it' (Mt.16:18).

Questions

1. What sort of pressure, if any, has been used to stop you going to church?

2. How is money used against the church today?

3. Why does the press usually only cover stories which are about scandal amongst Christians?

Personalities

Xerxes (verse 6) Also known in Hebrew as *Ahasuerus*, he was one of the Persian rulers. The beginning of his reign (verse 6) refers to the point when he came to power (486–465 BC). Verses 6–23

should be seen as a quick look forward because Darius came well before Xerxes, who is the king who features in the story of Esther in the book of that name.

Artaxerxes (verse 7) Artaxerxes I reigned over the Persian Empire 464–424 BC, the period during which the story of Ezra and Nehemiah takes place. The period mentioned in verse 7 is not given but by referring to Nehemiah 1:1–3 it would seem to be in the twentieth year of his reign, around 446 BC, that is several years prior to his decree dated 444 BC (Ne.2:1–8).

He was nicknamed 'long-armed' by the Greeks because his right arm was reputed to be longer than his left. He was King Xerxes' son.

Ashurbanipal (verse 10) 'Osnappar' is an alternative use of the name in the Aramaic. He became king of Assyria in 699 BC on the death of his father Esarhaddon until he himself died in about 626 BC. It is thought that he was the king who liberated Manasseh from captivity in Nineveh (2 Ch.33:13). He captured the city of Susa in 645 BC (see note on verse 9).

Ashurbanipal has since become famous as a result of excavations at Nineveh by George Smith from AD 1854 to 1873 which revealed his great collection of literature on 30,000 clay tablets.

Geography

Elamites of Susa (verse 9) Susa was a fortified town in south-west Persia, also mentioned in Nehemiah 1:1. It was the capital of Elam, a land covering the plain of Khuzistan and thrived until captured by Ashurbanipal who exiled many of its people to Samaria and sent Israelites to Elam (Is.11:11).

Elam is said to be the son of Shem in Genesis 10:22. Darius I built a palace at Susa which was restored by Artaxerxes I when it fell into disrepair. The site of the city has been excavated by a number of archaeologists, particularly the French, and the famous *Stele of Hammurapi*'s law codes was discovered here.

Biblical terms

We are under obligation (verse 14) The literal
translation used here is interesting; 'we eat the salt
of the palace'. The Jewish custom of eating salt can
mean the binding of an oath or covenant by eating a
meal together savoured with salt (Lv.2:13; Nu.18:19;
2 Ch.13:5).

Ezra 5:1–5

Words and work

God's word can never be suppressed and he will be with those who do his will.

The work had come to a standstill and the builders were laid off but it was not for long. God always has someone waiting for the right moment to get things moving again and Jerusalem at the time of Ezra was no exception. Now it was time to get back to work.
Haggai and Zechariah, the two prophets, make their appearance in order to encourage the people to get on with rebuilding the Temple. Much of what they actually said and did is covered by the books of Haggai and Zechariah in the section of the Bible known as 'the minor prophets'. It was a time of political upheaval: a period when people were in danger of forgetting the commission they had been given to restore the Temple and looking after their own personal comfort. It was time to put words into consolidated action: Zerubbabel and Jeshua set the example. There is no use in telling others what to do unless you are prepared to get your own hands dirty and so the prophets joined in as well (verse 2).

God had given permission but as yet the civil authorities had not received the paperwork and so Tattenai, the provincial governor asks, 'Who authorised you to rebuild this temple and restore this structure?' (verse 3). There appears to have been no hostility about his enquiry, but as far as he was concerned he had not been informed through the proper channels and so was checking things out for himself. Like so many administrators he wanted to ensure he had covered himself in case there was any backlash from higher up.

However, God had his eye on things (verse 5) and the work continued. The phrase is worth noting because the more normal phrase used was 'the hand of God'. The phrase, 'The eye of God', is more unusual (Jb.36:7; Pss.33:18; 34:15) but it was reassuring to know that God was watching. It may also be a play on words because the Persian civil servant inspectors were known at that time as 'the king's eye'.

Sometimes people forget and think God comes and goes, which is why Jesus told the story of the Father noticing the sparrow which falls, and having such an eye for detail that even the hairs on our heads are numbered (Mt.12:29–30; Lk.12:6–7).

The situation was difficult because it seemed that God had given permission to continue rebuilding but the civil authorities, as yet, had not: there was still an order out that the work should cease (4:21). Encouraged by the two prophets, Haggai and Zechariah, the Jews in Jerusalem made a hard choice: God's authority was final, this order had come right from the top! He was in charge of everything, including the civil authorities. Words must now be translated into work.

The conflict between religious and state interests is also seen in the New Testament at Jesus' trial when Pilate struggled with similar issues of earthly and heavenly authority (Jn.18:29–38).

Throughout the centuries Christians have wrestled with the same issue: 'What do you do when God tells you one thing and the civil authorities another?' and 'How can you be sure that it is God who is speaking?' Neither of these questions have easy answers and people have died believing God's will was more important than that of state or even church government.

What is certain is that if we talk too much nothing gets done. Without vision people tend to form committees. People of vision are always marked by their eagerness to turn words into work under the certain conviction that the will of God will never be suppressed.

Questions

1. *If you had to work out the percentage of time you spent talking and the time you spent working what would be the split?*

2. *If you lived in a country where attending church was illegal and death was the penalty for breaking the law what would you do, honestly?*

3. *Even in the church there is often more talk than there is action. This has resulted in people in the church getting on with a task without church approval (refusal to pay certain taxes, civil disobedience and violent resistance for example). How do you think Christians should respond in the light of Paul's comments in Romans 13:16?*

Personalities

Haggai (verse 1) We do not know very much about Haggai although it seems certain from the text that he was well known at the time. His name is taken from the Hebrew word for *a sacred festival*. It is by no means clear whether he had been in exile or whether he had stayed in Judah.

What we do know is that he prophesied to God's people calling on them to stop looking after their own houses and neglecting the house of God, the Temple (Hg.1:4–6). He is called to speak on behalf of God at a time when there was a need to stir up the national conscience.

Within a three-month period in 520 BC he spoke four times and then seems to disappear from public view. However, his words were certainly effective as they did stir people into action.

Zechariah (verse 1) We know little more about Zechariah than we do of Haggai. His name means 'God remembers' and he is listed as one of the prophets who returned from the exile (Ne.12:16).

In the book of Zechariah he calls the nation to restore moral standards (7:8–13; 8:16–17). His ministry began two months after that of Haggai and continued until 518 BC. Zechariah, like Haggai, sees the restoring of the Temple as the mark of the beginning of a new golden age in Israel's history and the hope of the coming of the messiah. He sees Jeshua and Zerubbabel as having an important part in this.

Tattenai (verse 3) He was the Persian governor of Samaria during the time of Darius and his name occurs not only in the Bible but also on a clay tablet, written in cuneiform (wedge-shaped writing), found in Babylon and dating from 5th June 502 BC (translated by A.T. Olmstead in 1944).

Ezra 5:6–17

Check it out!

Whenever the truth is questioned it is important to discover the facts.

Tattenai sent a letter to the king in order to inform him of events and establish the facts before making any moves (verses 7–10). He includes the response given to him by the Jewish leaders when asked on whose authority work had restarted (verses 11–16).

The word 'elders' is used in verse 9 but the more usual wording for leaders in Ezra is 'the heads of families' (Ezr.1:5; 3:12; 4:3) which suggests these are Tattenai's actual words rather than a précis by Ezra. The list of names of the elders is not included (verse 10) and could mean one of two things: either they refused to give one, or it was a repeat list of those mentioned in Ezra 2.

The main appeal of the elders was their claim that a former king, Cyrus, had given permission for the Temple to be restored. The king's word was law and the laws of the Persians and the Medes were unalterable. Darius would be under obligation to allow the work to continue if the truth could be established. In his letter Tattenai asks for a search to be made in the record office in order to discover the facts.

Too often mistakes are made because someone is not in possession of all the facts: Tattenai was taking no chances. If Christians are seeking God's will it is important to be aware of all the facts in a situation. Otherwise folk can go charging into a situation like 'a bull in a china shop' and cause more harm than good as a result. Tattenai resorted to the Persian archives and the king for his authority. Believers have access to the highest authority, God's word, and so it is important to ensure we have the backing of Scripture before embarking on what we believe is a God-given task. Sometimes the phrase, 'God told me', is used as a 'shut-up' bid by an individual in the church to override the authority of the leadership. There may be a valid basis for their claim but the only way to be sure of the truth is to test it. In the words of John, 'test the spirits to see whether they are from God' (1 Jn.4:1). Weigh it, pray it, search the Scriptures, in other words check it out.

Questions

1. What ways do you have of checking out what God is saying to you as against your own personal desires?

2. How do creeds (statements of belief) help the church guard the truth?

3. When different churches claim to have searched the Bible for answers and come to different conclusions is there any other way of discovering the truth?

Biblical terms

Large stones (verse 8) The words used here can be translated in a number of ways but the root word means to roll so they could be called 'the rolling stones'. That is, they were too large to carry so they had to be rolled.

Geography

Chaldean (verse 12) Chaldea is the name given to the southern part of Babylon and is also used of the semi-nomadic tribe who lived in the wilderness region between north Arabia and the Persian Gulf. The great city of Ur is referred to as Ur of the Chaldeans (Gn.11:31). Nebuchadnezzar was from the Chaldean tribe, but also king of Babylon, and so the term is widened to mean all of Babylon (Is.13:19; 47:1, 5; 48:14, 20).

Ezra 6:1-12

Mentioned in despatches

It might seem easier just to ignore those in authority when there is conflict of interest but it is always best to try and work through the system if you can.

Darius put his researchers to work in the treasury archives to discover if there was any truth in the claim made by the Jewish leaders in Jerusalem and a scroll was found. The rebuilding of the Temple was also mentioned in despatches. In fact, even the building specifications were included, so there could be no argument (verses 3–5). Darius sent a letter back to Tattenai and proclaimed it a royal decree, informing him that there should be no interference and that the work should continue with all expenses paid by the royal treasury (verse 8). Just to make the point that he meant business Darius included a gruesome description of the fate of anyone foolish enough to ignore his decree (verses 11–12).

Imagine the way that Haggai and Zechariah would have felt when the news reached Jerusalem. They had proclaimed God's word in faith, convinced they were right. They had endured the administrative frustrations of civil government, going through all the correct procedures, and they had discovered that patience really is a virtue, as well as a gift from God.

There may have been a temptation to take short cuts but they resisted and did everything decently and in order. Now they not only had the king's consent, but cash to cover costs from the royal treasury as well!

Many years later, and speaking in the context of false prophecy and persecution Jesus said, 'He who stands firm to the end will be saved' (Mt.24:13; Mk.13:13). Plodding through civil structure and administration to achieve the purposes of God can be one of the most irritating experiences in life so why bother? Well, apart from the point that impatience is not glorifying God, take the example of the patience of the Jews, not only in this story but over thousands of years. They have consistently proved that patient plodding works. It may not be easy but you get there in the end.

In the short term persecution and opposition to Christian activities sometimes seem to succeed. However, apart from patience, there is a way to overcome resistance to God's work. Peter Marshall, a Scottish minister who worked in Washington, USA, once said, 'Prayer moves the hand that controls the universe'. The builders of the Temple must have been a people of prayer because Darius was keen to be mentioned in despatches to God. He asked in his letter to Tattenai that the priests 'pray for the well-being of the king and his sons' (verse 10). So he must have been impressed with their faith. Whenever you are involved in difficulties make sure it gets mentioned in despatches.

Questions

1. When you feel everything and everyone is against you because of your faith what do you do in order to cope?

2. When you have prayed for something or someone specific what have been the longest and shortest times before you received an answer?

3. Church leaders in this country are sometimes criticized for not giving enough of a moral and ethical lead to the nation. How should they respond?

Geography

Ecbatana (verse 2) This is the Greek name for Achmetha and was the capital of Media (modern day Hamadan). It was on the old caravan route through the Zagros mountains and was well known for its cold winters but very pleasant summers, with the result that Cyrus chose it to be his summer home, as did a number of the Persian kings.

Cyrus's decree of 538 BC, giving permission to rebuild the Temple, was kept in the library here. Herodotus, the Greek historian, describes the city[4].

Weights and Measures

Cubits (verse 3) The NIV gives the measurement of the Temple in feet but originally the measurement was given as 'cubits'. This measurement was not as accurate as modern forms as it was based on human proportions which of course vary from one person to another. So 'a span' was the measurement from
the thumb to little fingertip spread; 'the cubit' was the distance from the elbow to the middle fingertip; and 'a rope', or 'fathom', was taken from one middle fingertip of one arm to the middle fingertip of the other when the arms were spread out.

The measurement given here is only approximate because a cubit can vary from about from about 17.7 inches to 20.5 inches.

Ezra 6:13–16

Prescription for joy

There is real joy in seeing God's will completed and knowing you are part of it is a real tonic.

Tattenai always followed orders. He had his instructions and there was no bad feeling so now he made sure that every assistance was available to ensure the Temple was completed (verse 14). The building work carried on and so did the preachers (verse 14) presumably during the tea breaks!

The hopes and dreams of those who had returned home so many years before were fulfilled as the Temple once again stood proudly over Jerusalem. It was completed on the third day of *Adar*. The month of Adar (verse 15) is twelfth in the Babylonian calendar and is the equivalent in time of February/March when late planting and the hoeing of flax took place. The Feast of Purim (celebrating the deliverance of God's people in the story of Esther) took place on the 13th–15th days of Adar.

The sixth year of the reign of Darius (verse 15) would be 515 BC, twenty-one years after the foundation of the Temple had been laid and about four and a-half years after Haggai had challenged the people to get on with building the Temple. The third day of the month is widely accepted now as 12th March 515 BC. This confirms Jeremiah's prophecy of freedom for the Israelites after seventy years (see chapter 1) from the Temple's destruction in 586 BC to restoration in 516 BC (the temple was completed on the third day of the new year 515 BC so this year would not be counted).

After the fall of Jerusalem, and the deportations of many of the Jews, maintaining their identity would have been a real problem. It would have been even more difficult when they returned home to discover that strangers from other lands had moved into the area in the mean time.

Rebuilding the Temple at Jerusalem was rather like raising the flag on a battleground when surrounded by the enemy. Now the Temple had been completed Jerusalem could once again be known as the Holy City and Jews from all over the Empire could look again to Jerusalem as the focus of their identity.

It was a place which would focus on the presence of God and where they could make pilgrimages with pride, knowing they belonged. The day the Temple was completed, twenty-one years after the foundation had been laid, was a real prescription for joy.

The foundation stone for the new temple was laid when Jesus became the capstone or cornerstone (1 Pet.2:7) and Peter reminds his readers that every believer is a living stone being built into the temple (1 Pet.2:5), a theme which occurs a number of times in the New Testament.

'In him the whole building is joined together and rises to become a holy temple in the LORD. And in him you too are being built together to become a dwelling in which God lives by his Spirit' (Eph.2:20–21; see also 1 Cor.3:16; 6:19; 2 Cor.6:16; Rev.3:12; 21:22).

Christians sometimes lose their identity as the people of God because the 'living temple' is not being built. God's prescription for real joy comes from raising the flag, lifting up the name of Jesus and carrying out the task he gave us all to do, to proclaim the Good News (Mt.28:19).

Commencing a new work can be exciting, continuing the task requires endurance, and completion of the work leads to joy and job satisfaction. It is a good prescription for joy in the power and presence of God.

Questions

1. Have you ever been involved in a project where you not only were in at the beginning, but also saw it finished? If so, how did you feel when it was completed?

2. Do you think it is possible to be a Christian without belonging to a church? If your answer is yes, where can that person feel they belong?

3. When will the building of the temple of Jesus Christ be completed?

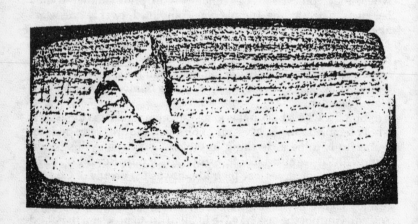

Fig. 4: The Cyrus Cylinder
(It records Cyrus's permission to exiles from the nations to return to their homes. It can be seen in the British Museum.)

Ezra 6:17–22

Cause for joy

Sacrificial giving to God and worship to him are a real cause for joy for the believer.

The feast of Passover was a memorial celebrating God's deliverance of his people from their first captivity in Egypt. Now it was cause for celebration for freedom, not only from slavery in Egypt but exile in Babylon. The 'cream on the cake' was the opportunity to celebrate the completion of the Temple as well. It was not quite on the same scale as the dedication of the first Temple built by Solomon because the nation was only just being re-established in the land. For instance, over 200 times as many animals were sacrificed at Solomon's Temple (compare verses 16–17 with 1 Ki.8:63). People had given generously to the building fund when they could have readily put a case forward for their own needs but did not.

It was not a question of how much was given but at what cost? This is reminiscent of the story of Jesus watching people putting their offerings into the Temple treasury. Jesus measured not by the amount given but the sacrifice involved. 'I tell you the truth, this poor widow has put more into the treasury than all the others. They all gave out of their wealth; but she, out of her poverty.' (Mk.12:43–44).

Celebration involved not only the giving of sacrifices but also total giving of each individual of themselves to God. This is what purification involved (verse 20): getting rid of anything in their lives which was not acceptable to God in order to give themselves completely to him. This meant they were truly free to celebrate and the result was a seven-day-long 'knees-up' because God filled them with joy (verse 22).

There was nothing cold and formal about this time of worship, God had made them glad! The Hebrew word which is used for 'joy' means 'enjoying yourself', or 'having a good time'. Some people might find it hard to imagine that God would give people the opportunity for a good time, a party atmosphere, in worship (for more on the two main Hebrew concepts of joy see the comments on Ne.8).

The story has much of the feel of a birthday party: a party where a lot of time and planning has gone into making sure everything goes according to plan. Where people have given almost beyond their ability to give because of their love for the one who is the reason for the celebration. The joy comes from the response of the person when they have opened the presents and joined in the party.

Jesus probably had something of this kind of merriment in mind when he spoke about the kingdom of God. He used parables which focused on banquets and weddings to explain that building the kingdom of God was a cause of real excitement for those who were prepared to make the effort (Mt.22:1–14; Lk.12:36; 14:15–23; 15:23–31).

Tony Campolo, an American preacher and sociologist says it well: 'The kingdom of God is a party!'

The point is well made in this passage that nothing comes from doing nothing, but giving personally of money, time and effort at a sacrificial level to God is ultimately a real cause for joy.

Questions

1. *What kind of experiences make you happy?*

2. *How do you discern the difference between greed and need in your life?*

3. *What can the worldwide church learn from this passage?*

Biblical terms

The Book of Moses (verse 18) and similar phrases ('the book of the covenant' and 'the Law of Moses') assume the reader is familiar with the rules and regulations of religious practice and community life as recorded in the first five books of the Bible (see Ex.29; Lv.8; Nu.3:5f; 8:5f).

Times and seasons

Passover (verse 19) The Passover in 516 BC was held in the second half of April (our calendar). 'The 14th day of the first month' is the fourteenth day of Nisan (March/April) – the word means 'sprouting' and it was the time of the barley harvest. Following this, from the 15th to the 21st day was the Feast of Unleavened Bread.

The *Feast of Passover* is described in Exodus 12:1–11, Leviticus 23:5–6 and Numbers 9:11. On the 13th day of Nisan each Jewish household searched to make sure that there was no unleavened bread anywhere in the house. A lamb or goat was taken to the Temple on the 14th day for sacrifice (about one animal for every ten to twelve people), the fat was burned and the blood spilled onto the altar. The carcass was normally then taken home and cooked. The ceremony that followed was a remembrance of the events leading up to the leaving of Egypt by the Israelites at the time of Moses and the Exodus (the going out). Jews today will sometimes call it the *Feast of Freedom*.

Feast of Unleavened Bread (verse 22) Instructions for the feast can be found in Exodus 12:15–20, Leviticus 23:6–8 and Numbers 28:17. The emphasis of this feast here is 'joy' (verses 16, 22; 2 Ch.30:21; see note on Ezr.3:12,13), to make clear that this is a very happy occasion.

The ceremony was enacted through a series of questions and answers led by the head of the household and prompted normally by the youngest articulate member of the family. In it they were reminded that the unleavened bread (bread made without yeast), bitter herbs and chutney symbolized the haste, the bitterness and the hard labour their ancestors had experienced in Egypt. Four cups of red wine were used to give thanks to God and only unleavened bread was eaten during that week.

Ezra 7:1–10

Man with a mission

God always has the right person for the right time in history to help his people.

The first two stages in God's incredible plan, as outlined in Ezra and Nehemiah, are now complete. His people have returned to the land and his Temple has been restored. The third stage begins in chapter 7 as Ezra, the man with a mission, comes onto the scene. His task? To begin to rebuild the people of God into a nation of spiritual power and purity for the sake of the glory of God.

This passage gives the reader background information regarding Ezra and his family tree. He arrives in Jerusalem sixty years after the period covered by chapter 6 in 458 BC. (Some do argue for a much later date, see 'Outlining the Issues'.) Ezra set out from the Jewish community in Babylon, with a letter from Artaxerxes I, to ensure that the Jews in Jerusalem and the surrounding area observe their religious laws in full. Ezra brought a significant number of people with him from Babylon (a journey of some 900 miles) to help in the task and also financial contributions for the Temple.

Until the exile the role of scribes were separate from that of priests, but Ezra was a scribe (teacher) as well as a priest, and probably advised King Artaxerxes on Jewish affairs. Scribes were also used as secretaries to write letters and legal documents, as well as keep records and accounts (Je.32:12; 36:26; 2 Ch.24:11). It was a financially rewarding profession which often followed on from father to son (1 Ch.2:55).

Ezra's role was going to be a tough one. He was expected to be a guardian of God's word, both a priest and a teacher of the Law (verse 6), devoted to its study and observance (verse 10). The king of Persia obviously had great faith in him because he gave him everything he asked for.

Twice in this short passage it is noted that everything went well for Ezra because 'God's hand was upon him' (verses 6,9). It is obvious to the reader that Ezra is the 'man of the moment', a man with a mission. To emphasize this the phrase, 'God's hand' is repeated later (8:18,22,31).

Throughout the Bible there is a pattern which demonstrates the fact that God always has the right person ready for the right time in history. Moses led the exodus, Joshua was prepared for conquering Canaan; when Saul's rule failed God had David ready and waiting in the wings.

Right through the Old Testament this pattern continued until God called his own Son to carry out the ultimate mission, to break the power of sin and death, to make it possible for a lost world to be reconciled to its Maker. Then after the resurrection came Peter, Paul, and many more men and women who have all been a part of God's incredible plan.

Most of those concerned did not think they were ready or fit for the job, but God used them anyway. Jeremiah comes close to understanding God's way when he writes of Israel, 'Like clay in the hand of the potter, so you are in my hand' (Je.18:6) and Paul brings a Christian perspective, 'Does not the potter have the right to make out of the same lump of clay some pottery for noble purposes and some for common use?' (Rom.9:21).

God always has the right person at the right place at the right time, even though the person often doesn't feel up to the task. But it is not a question of what can I do for God? It is more a case of what God can do with me?

> **Questions**
>
> 1. How has God used you and did you feel you were the right person for the task?
>
> 2. Why do you think Ezra was not with the first group of Jews to return?
>
> 3. Who would you say is God's man or woman of the moment in the world today?

Personalities

Ezra (verse 1) is the Aramaic equivalent of the Hebrew name Azariah which means the 'Lord has helped'. His family tree listed here makes it clear that he has a good priestly pedigree but he is not listed as a high priest. According to tradition, Ezra is also attributed with the authorship of Chronicles, Ezra and Nehemiah.

Ezra is popularly known as 'Ezra the scribe', although the word used here is 'teacher' (verses 6,11): for some reason which is not obvious the NIV translates the Hebrew word used here as 'teacher' and yet, referring to the same person (Ezra) and using the same Hebrew word it translates 'scribe' in Nehemiah (8:1,4,9,13; 12:26, 36). It can also mean 'secretary'. By the time of Ezra the Hebrew word, *Saphar*, from the root 'to count' or 'to recount', had come to mean 'one who is skilled in reading and interpreting religious writings and law' (that is, a court scholar).

Times and seasons

Seventh year of Artaxerxes (verse 8) That is, 458 BC, although there are those who argue that the Artaxerxes mentioned is actually Artaxerxes II who ruled from 404 to 359 BC (an argument used to suggest that Nehemiah arrived in Jerusalem before Ezra because we know Nehemiah arrived in 445[5]; see

'Outlining the Issues'). The majority of scholars take for granted that the date is according to the Persian reign of kings which runs from Spring to Spring or *Nisan* to *Nisan* as in the Jewish calendar.

Fifth month of the seventh year (verse 8) – and the first day of the first month (verse 9)

The first day of the first month, *Nisan*, corresponds to 8th April and the first day of the fifth month, *Ab*, is the equivalent of 4th August. Ab is July/August, the time of the olive harvest and the beginning of the dates and summer figs.

So Ezra and his group began their journey in the spring, two days before Passover, and followed the pattern of the first exodus from Egypt by eating the unleavened bread on the road (Ex.12:39); they arrived in mid-summer exactly fourteen weeks later.

Ezra 7:11–26

In the name of the King

God places rulers in authority so we should not be surprised to see kings being used to provide the way forward for his will.

The significance of Ezra's part in God's plan is emphasized in the fact that not only had the king given him what he had asked for, but he had credentials in the form of a letter in the name of the king. In the letter Ezra is recognized by the king as a teacher of the law of God (verse 12) and he is sent by the king to Jerusalem to check up on observance of the Law of God (verse 14). 'The Law of God, which is in your hand' (verse 14) did not mean that he literally had a scroll of the Law, or Torah in his hand. 'In his hand' was a figure of speech meaning that it was in his care and he understood it: hence the title given to Ezra in verse 11.

What is amazing is that the non-Jewish king tells Ezra to take money from the state treasury as well as the freewill offering to finance his work (verse 16). The king asks him to be responsible not only for the Law of God, but the law of the king as well (verses 25–26). The appointment of magistrates and judges on behalf of the king would be very much in line with the Torah (Dt.16:18).

Some have debated whether Ezra had the king's authority over civil issues as well as the sacred and have suggested that really they were one and the same. The evidence suggests that as Jews living in Babylon had been subject to civil law for some years it is perfectly reasonable to suppose the king gave him authority over both civil and religious law.

There are other examples like the Egyptian 'satrap' who was given a similar brief by Darius in 519 BC[6] (see note on Satraps in 8:32–36).

Other Jews in Babylon had been given responsibility in affairs of state including Daniel and his friends and Esther, a Jew, became a queen.

There have often been tensions between religion and politics, church and state, but then there have always been Christians who have also been involved in both. Like Ezra they could claim to be doing their job in the name of God and in the name of the king.

The difficulty has always been to know where to draw the line between the law of the land and the Law of God.

In Jesus' day the religious leaders tried to trap him on a number of occasions by getting him into a debate on this very same controversy. What belonged to God and what belonged to the civil ruler (Mt.22:15–21)? When religious law and civil law were both broken, which had priority over the other? If Jesus claimed to be a king, was he infringing the authority of the Roman Empire?

The point of the passage is that God is in control. He has authority, even over rulers, and so can and does use them to carry out his will. How else did Ezra manage to obtain such an encouraging letter from Artaxerxes?

That is why Jesus could reply to one trick question, 'Give to Caesar what is Caesar's, and to God what is God's' (Mt.22:21).

Hence we continue to acknowledge the temporal authority of civil leadership by including prayers for our leaders in church prayer books.

The key to Ezra's mission and to ours is that whatever is done is done with divine backing and authority. When we act is it with the full assurance that we have permission to speak in the name of the King?

> ## Questions
>
> 1. *There is a saying 'politics and religion don't mix'. What do you think?*
>
> 2. *If Christians are appointed as legal judges have they the right to stand in judgment over others when the Bible tells us we must not?*
>
> 3. *Can you be a Christian and a politician?*

Biblical terms

King of kings (verse 12) During the time of the Persian kings this was a title frequently used to address them (Ezk.26:7; Dn.2:37) and is found in a number of Persian documents from this period. It also came into use in New Testament times via the Roman Empire; normally a title given to the overall ruler it is now used of Jesus (1 Tim.6:15; Rev.17:14;19:16).

Weights and measures

Talents, cors and baths (verse 22) It is not easy to give the exact modern equivalent of these measurements because of the flexibility in definition (see Ezr.6:3). For example we know that the Temple of Solomon had a large tank known as the 'sea of bronze' which measured 10 cubits in diameter and 5 cubits in depth (1 Ki.7:23). But as we have already noted, a cubit varied in length according to who was doing the measuring. The tank contained 2,000 baths (3,000 in 2 Ch.4:5). A bath was a measure of liquids such as water, wine and oil (1 Ki.7:26,28; 2 Ch.2:9) and 100 baths was approximately 607 gallons.

A hundred talents of silver weighed approximately 3.75 tons. The 'cor' was used as a measure of weight for flour, wheat and barley (1 Ki.5:2), and a hundred cors of wheat was around 650 bushels.

History

Imprisonment (verse 26) was a form of punishment that was virtually unknown in Old Testament Law and the closest parallel is temporary detention (Lv.24:12; Nu.15:34). Joseph was put in prison but that was in Egypt (Gn.39:20–23); Samson was imprisoned by the Philistines (Jdg.16:21) but in Judah a guardroom would act only as a temporary prison for Jeremiah (Je.32:2,8,12). However, Micaiah was put on a diet of bread and water in prison until the king returned in peace (I Ki.22:27; 2 Ch.18:26).

Ezra 7:27–28

Thanks a lot!

It is important not to take God for granted but to give him thanks always.

These few verses form a classic Hebrew benediction in the form of a psalm of praise. It thanks God for his goodness and then gives an account of what he has done. It is a pattern which is followed again and again in the book of Psalms.

Ezra makes it clear here why he is God's 'man of the moment'. He never forgets to give him thanks for the way he was working through the king and his officials and in Ezra's own life. He happily acknowledges that he has only achieved what he has through the provision and intervention of the Lord: a God who can move a foreign king's heart to be concerned over Jerusalem and its temple. Armed with the knowledge that God is on his side Ezra prepares to lead a caravan of Jewish leaders down to Jerusalem.

The NIV's translation of the Hebrew into 'his good favour' (verse 28) is a pity because the meaning has been weakened. The word *Chesed* used for 'good favour' is normally translated 'care', 'loving kindness', 'mercy', or 'covenant love'.

Recognizing God's unchanging love and giving thanks for it is a constant theme in the Psalms. Daniel was a man of prayer who was known for the way he regularly gave thanks to God (Dn.6:10).

The frustration is that human nature being what it is people are usually far quicker at complaining when things are not right than in giving thanks when God's goodness is apparent. Jesus made this point when he healed the ten lepers. They were all quick enough to ask for help but only one bothered to come back and thank Jesus for what he had done (Lk.17:11–19).

I remember as a child that I loved getting presents for my birthday or for Christmas. What I was not so fond of was sitting down to write 'thank you letters' afterwards. My mother pointed out that if I didn't then I should not expect family and friends to send me anything. The principle is the same in the Christian life; if I take God for granted do I have any right to expect him to help me all the time? Surely it is a Christian's duty when he or she recognizes God's provision in life to say, 'Thanks a lot.'

Questions

1. What has God done for you today?

2. If you think about the prayers you have prayed recently, how many were 'I wants', and how many were 'thank yous'?

3. Why do people complain far quicker than they say thank you?

Biblical terms

To bring honour (verse 27) This phrase is better translated 'to adorn' or 'to beautify the Temple'. It is a phrase which is used on a number of occasions in Isaiah with specific reference to the Temple and God's people (Is.55:5; 60:7,9, 13). God himself is always the subject of the word and used here it can either refer to the offerings in the Temple or the actual restoration of the Temple.

His good favour (verse 28) is derived from an Old Testament word for the stork, a bird devoted in its care for its young and so 'the devoted or unchanging love of God for his people' is the intention behind the word. The most powerful illustration of its use is in the story of God's love for Israel in the book of Hosea (Ho.2:19;4:1; 6:4,6;10:12;12:6). The same word occurs in Ezra (3:11;9:9) and Nehemiah (1:5; 9:17, 32; 13:14–22).

Ezra 8:1–14

Roll of honour

The list of names is a reminder that everyone of us is known by name to God.

All of the families listed here, with the possible exception of Joab's (verse 9) are rejoining relatives who had returned eighty years earlier (Ezr.2:3–15; cf 8:3–14). In Ezra 2:6 Joab's family tree is recorded directly from Pahath-Moab (this is not a family name but means 'governor of Moab') through Jeshua and Joab. Whereas here in verse 4 the main family is mentioned and Joab's family line is listed as a separate group. It may be because this is an easier way of breaking down the numbers involved or to single out Joab as different from the one mentioned in Ezra 2:6, it is not clear which.

The roll of honour breaks down into three main groups, similar to other lists of names in Ezra and Nehemiah. First are the priests (verse 2) followed by the noble families (verses 2–3), and then those from ordinary families who make up the bulk of the caravan (verses 3–14). Some of the family names are also mentioned in the second chapter of Ezra which suggests that those who had gone back to Jerusalem on the first Return had sent word to Babylon, and now more members of their families were setting out to join them.

The whole caravan, including men, women and children would have probably numbered somewhere around 5,000 people. The way that Ezra had managed to recruit this many people suggests that a new sense of purpose and the presence of God was beginning to burn in the hearts of his people. The first Return must have been compared with the exodus of Moses and the people from Egypt. Those families whose names were recorded in Ezra 2 had their names on the roll of honour, now others were following their example.

Something akin to the pioneering spirit of the people groups who left Europe to begin a new life in America or Australia in the nineteenth century must have gripped the Israelites. This excitement and desire to return to the promised land would affect the Jews of Russia in the latter part of the last century. It would gather momentum as Jews from France, Britain and Europe, then the rest of the world, began to experience the same feelings that God was calling them home to the land of Israel, until Israel was a nation once again with Jerusalem as its capital.

One thing worth noting is the fact that there are no lists of families in Babylon other than those who return to Israel. There is no criticism of which group returned when, it was only important that they returned. Then their names were placed on the roll of honour.

This event has some similarity with the Christian call to return to a right relationship with God through Jesus Christ. It doesn't matter when someone returns to God, only that they do return, then their names can be included on the roll of honour: the Lamb's book of life (Phil.4:3; Rev.3:5; 13:8; 17:8; 20:12, 15; 22:19).

Questions

1. Why do churches sometimes put people's names on memorial plaques in their buildings?

2. Do you think it is easier to be a Christian if you already have family in the church?

3. When the prodigal son returned home (Lk.15:11–32) why did the brother and the father have different attitudes?

Biblical terms

The last ones (verse 13) This phrase has caused some puzzlement to scholars because the main pattern of listing the families is changed at this point. Some have suggested that this line was added later, others that it just meant 'and finally'. There is another possibility, this family could have been making *aliyah*.

Aliyah is a Hebrew word which literally means 'going up' and was used in a number of ways: going up to the lectern to read a portion of Scripture; of an upper room; but it is also used to mean returning to Palestine. The phrase is used in Ezra 1:3 and 5 in just this way. The call 'to go up' and possess the land is the same word (Dt.9:23).

So 'the last ones' could well be the last members of that family to make their *aliyah* back to Judah, as against the large numbers of Jews who never returned.

Ezra 8:15–20

Down by the riverside

Being where God wants you to be means being prepared to do your duty.

For three days Ezra set about gathering the people together ready for the long trek home. The assembly point was a canal (verse 15) and the river Euphrates had a number of canals leading off it. They were not 'narrow-boat' canals but were drainage canals, used to defend the fields against flooding. Both the Tigris and Euphrates rivers were subject to flooding in the early summer and waiting for the waters to go down would have meant it was too late for seed sowing. In order to tackle the problem a whole series of canals or dykes were dug for drainage. The same word is used in Psalm 74:15 referring to 'streams' and Psalm 93:3 where the word used is 'flood' (RSV), or 'sea' (NIV), reflecting the idea of water that comes and goes. I wonder if this is where the hymn writer got the idea for the hymn, 'Shall we gather at the river?'?

When he came to check out the mix of people who made up the caravan Ezra discovered a shortage of Levites (verse 15). As one of the primary reasons for the return was to build up the Jews of Israel in their relationship with God it was vital to have a reasonable number of religious leaders. There were priests (verse 15), men of learning (verse 16), temple servants (verse 20), but no Levites. Building the Temple was one thing but trying to maintain a believing body of people without proper leadership was quite another. Ezra knew that they must be prepared, even though the hand of God was on them (verse 18).

Sometimes believers faced with practical difficulties fall into the trap of saying, 'God is with us so everything will work out fine', but make no attempt to do anything themselves.

Ezra seems to have worked on the principle that 'the Lord helps those who help themselves', as we shall see later.

Part of real spirituality is to ensure practical details are dealt with in a realistic rather than fatalistic way. Ezra ensured he had everything and everyone he needed before he was prepared to embark on the mission God had called him to.

The motto of the Scout movement is 'Be Prepared', and one of the promises they make is to do their duty. That was the model of Ezra and the call to Christians today: God is with us but don't see that as an opportunity to opt out of responsibility – be prepared to do your duty.

Questions

1. What do you think might have happened if Ezra had set off, failing to notice that he had no Levites?

2. Do you know people who leave everything to God to sort out without making any effort themselves? What happens?

3. How should the church ensure an eye for detail as well as carrying out its commission?

Geography

Ahava (verse 15) No-one knows for certain exactly where Ahava is, but the most likely answer is that it was situated close to the beginning of one of the caravan trading routes leading to the west.

The Greek geographer Strabo (1st century BC) has identified it with Scenae near Babylon, but even if he was wrong it cannot be far from there. Ezra only camped at Ahava for three days, which was enough time for the leaders of the party to go back to Babylon to encourage thirty-eight of the Levite community there to join the group.

Casiphia (verse 17) Again it is not possible to pinpoint this location other than it must have been close to Babylon. Iddo (verse 17) must have been a man of some importance for Ezra to send to him for help. So we may assume that Casiphia would have had a significant Jewish community and, with the mention of temple servants, possibly its own temple.

There were certainly at least two temples serving the Jewish community at this time, one at Elephantine, is referred to in the *Elephantine papyri*, the other at Leontopolis is mentioned by Josephus the Jewish historian. As both were in Egypt it is reasonable to assume that they had their Babylonian counterparts.

Ezra 8:21–31

Fasting and faith

Prayer and fasting are part of seeking God's will and purpose and help those who believe to go forward in faith.

At the Ahava Canal everything from the practical planning to the spiritual preparation was being organized – or was it? Ezra did not feel able to ask for the king's protection because he had made it clear that God was looking after them (verse 22). It was really a case of faith without works is dead. Ezra could not claim God was on his side if he was not prepared to prove it by his actions. This is probably why he proclaimed the fast (verse 21).

Fasting is only mentioned three times in Ezra/Nehemiah (Ezr.8:21–23; Ne.1:4; 9:1. Each time there was a direct link between fasting and conversation with God, and it normally meant abstaining from food and drink for a time. In this context it is preparatory to the request for a safe journey for the families and security of their belongings as they set out from Babylon to Jerusalem. There were set fast days during the year such as the 'Day of Atonement' or 'Yom Kippur' (Lev.16:29,31; 23:27–32). Additionally, there were one-off fasts for groups and individuals such as the examples found in Ezra and Nehemiah.

Fasting was used to express sorrow over sin and misfortune as well as displaying humility before God and people. Often fasting was perceived as a way of beginning to discover God's will for a particular situation, but there was always the warning that it was a waste of time if right living did not accompany it (Is.58:3–12; Mt.6:16–18).

In the Matthew account it is interesting to note that Jesus assumes that fasting is a part of the normal spiritual life. He does not say, '*If* you fast', but, '*When* you fast' (verse 16).

Ezra needed to be sure of God's will if they were to have a safe journey (verse 21), often translated 'a smooth journey', especially in view of the large amount of valuables they would be carrying with them (verses 25–27).

The literal words used are 'a straight road' which is interesting when you compare it with Isaiah's and John the Baptist's words (Is.40:3–4; Mk.1:3). The saying 'straight' or 'crooked' has something of the sense of this in describing someone as good or bad.

I feel sorry for the priests because they were given the specific responsibility of guarding the gifts for the Temple, not some strong and armed fighting men: although the responsibility probably improved their inclination to fast and pray!

True to form, being prepared to do his duty, and always practical in his eye for essentials, Ezra assisted the priests over any temptation to help themselves to the Temple treasure by weighing it out before handing it over (verses 25–27). He would weigh it again when they arrived in Jerusalem (verse 33). The fasting and faith were rewarded because God protected them from bandits along the way (verse 31).

Ezra demonstrates an important fact for Christians: being spiritual does not mean being naive or taken for a fool.

At the same time it is essential that faith is in God and not human institutions. I like the old saying, 'We trust the Lord, everybody else pays cash'. Know God's will then do it, and in order to be certain follow the model given by Ezra: fasting and faith.

Questions

1. How can someone with specific dietary needs for example a diabetic) fast without being irresponsible?

2. Why does going without food help people focus on God?

3. Should the church encourage fasting as a regular part of worship today?

Biblical terms

You...are consecrated to the LORD (verse 28) Consecrated is another word for holy. The Hebrew word *qodesh* means 'sacred', 'set apart' (for a purpose), 'dedicated to' or 'for', 'consecrated', 'holy', 'sanctified'. The word implies something or someone who is free from defilement or impurity (Ezr.3:5;

Ne.3:1; 8:9,10,11; 10:39; 12:47; 13:22). With it comes the expectation of being ceremonially clean in order to come into the presence of God (Lv.16:4,16–33).

Guard them carefully (verse 29) 'Keep them and stay awake' is how the literal Hebrew is expressed: anyone who has had to stay awake all night will have some insight into this meaning. Psalm 121:4 reminds us that God is always on guard, he does not sleep but watches over his people.

Times and seasons

Twelfth of the first month (verse 31) See back to the notes on Ezra 7:9.

Ezra 8:32-36

Return and rest

No-one is expected to keep going non-stop – rest is just as important as action.

Ezra and his party had waited three days at Ahava (verse 15), now they rested for three days at the end of their journey (verse 32). Was it possible that there is a link of a devotional nature here? That they waited not only for the Levites, but also to follow the pattern of the first exodus (compare Ezr.8:15 and the notes on Ezr.7:9)?

If so, then it is also feasible that if we go by the *Book of Jubilees* calendar (a book which gives a chronology of the main events of Israel's history to the day of the week, discovered at Qumran among the writings known as the *Dead Sea Scrolls*) then they arrived back on the eve of the sabbath (the day of rest), the same day of the week that Joshua had entered the land of Canaan, when he also paused for three days (Jos.3:1–2). As a result it would not be possible to deliver up the valuables they had brought with them to the priest at Jerusalem for three days.

This apart, three days was regarded as a normal rest period during this time (Ezr.10:8; Ne.2:11) and would be reasonable if you have to find food and shelter for around 5,000 fellow travellers.

There is a warning in Psalm 127:2 to workaholics: working all hours without proper rest is a waste of time because it is not God's intention. Even Jesus emphasized the need to take time for rest and relaxation (Mt.11:28; 26:45; Mk.6:31). People sometimes feel guilty about taking time to rest and relax but at the end of work it is not only in order, but an order from God.

Without proper rest after the Return Ezra, and the people with him, would not have been in a fit state to continue the task God had set before them. The message has not changed – rest is as important as action.

Questions

1. *How do you discern the difference between rest and being lazy?*

2. *Why do you think it is that some people never seem to take time to relax?*

3. *Does the church set a good example in maintaining a balance between meetings for the sake of meetings or doing nothing?*

Personalities

Meremoth (verse 33) The son of Uriah and belonging to the Hakkoz family he is also mentioned in Nehemiah 3:4–21. The Hakkoz family was one of those which, on the first return, were not able to prove they were of good Jewish stock (Ezr.2:59–63).

Obviously someone must have sorted something out because now one of the leading priests is from this family.

Jozabad (verse 33) He is also a descendant of one of the families involved in the first return (Ezr.2:40) and was an overseer of the outside work on the Temple (Ne.11:15).

Personnel

Satraps (verse 36) The Persian Empire was made up of twenty-eight regions and twenty of these were subject states called *satrapies* according to the Greek historian Herodotus. The word *satrap* comes from a Persian root meaning 'protector of the kingdom'. They had the authority to mint their own silver coins and each one was divided up into *eparchies* which were controlled by civil or military governors. These were split even smaller for the purpose of taxation and land control.

The *satrap* or governor had absolute civil authority as well as a fair amount of military clout. In order to avoid this leading to abuse of the position, in terms of greed or desire for more power, Darius appointed a local army chief who was directly answerable to him. Both the local tax collector and the satrap's secretary were also accountable directly to the king. Then just to ensure there was no threat to the good order of the Persian Empire someone close to the king, a high official or family member would drop in unannounced on the satrapies to make spot checks.

Ezra 9:1–7

Crisis of faith

No-one can serve two masters, it only leads to conflict.

Ezra chapters 9 and 10 form one complete section
and deals with the issue of compromising relationships amongst the Jews. The people had returned to
a confusing climate in which it was hard to discover
their identity. On the one hand there was a political
structure which involved people from other nations
and demanded their participation. On the other hand there was a
religious institution which also made demands on their loyalty to
its requirements. The only way many had coped with this crisis of
identity was to compromise, and compromise always seems to lead
to conflict.

The leaders in Jerusalem obviously had a guilty conscience about
the situation because soon after Ezra's arrival in the city they came
and told him (rather like a child who has done wrong who takes
the initiative and informs the parent before it is found out). Ezra's
reaction was nothing if not dramatic. 'I tore my tunic...pulled hair
from my head...' (verse 3). Behaviour of this kind was an expected
reaction to personal pain and to bereavement (2 Sa.13:19; 2 Ki.22:11;
Job 1:20; Ezk.7:18). Tearing of clothes was a Jewish modification
of going naked, as people of other nations might do in the same

circumstances. Nakedness was viewed by Jewish religious law as a lack of dignity and seen as a mark of shame (Gn.9:23; Ezk.16:39) or extreme poverty (Job 24:10) but tearing one's clothes was acceptable.

Men clipping their beards or shaving their heads in times of mourning was frowned on and priests were not expected to trim their beards (Lv.19:27; 21:5; Dt.14:1). The only parallel with Ezra's behaviour is when Nehemiah pulled out the hair of some of the men of Judah as a punishment (Ne.13:25). One of the Hebrew words for 'elder' literally means someone capable of growing a beard, so to remove facial hair was symbolic of taking away authority (see Ezra 10:6). Ezra's act was typical of 'prophetic symbolism', usually an act of extreme behaviour to make a significant impact on God's people in times of apathy or ignorance (2 Sa.19:24; Is.20:1–4, Ezk. 4 and 5).

Ezra records, 'I fell on my knees with my hands spread out' (verse 5). This was not the only position for prayer in the Old Testament (Ex.9:29; 1 Ki.8:22; Is.1:15). It was also permissible to pray standing (1 Sa.1:26), kneeling (1 Ki.8:54), hands lifted up (Ne.8:6), sitting (1 Ch.17:16) or even flat on one's face (1 Ch.21:16). Praying on his knees, for Ezra, was a sign of submission (Ps.95:6; Dn.6:10). What he says makes it clear that he viewed their guilt as his guilt because he talks about, 'our sins' (verse 6) and, 'our guilt' (verse 7). Compromise had led to conflict and a crisis of faith. His attitude was not a condescending judgment but reaction out of corporate accountability.

We can learn from Ezra's response by resisting the temptation to look down on other Christians who have been caught in this trap and recognize that, as a part of the body of Christ, we have to talk about our sins and our guilt – not just theirs.

Jesus recognized the problem and proclaimed, 'No man can serve two masters: for either he will hate the one, and love the other; or else he will be devoted to one and despise the other' (Mt.6:24; Lk.16:13).

Anything which gets between the Lord and a believer is idolatry and the second commandment clearly condemned this practice (Ex.20:4). When people attempt to water down the requirements of the Christian life compromise will produce conflict – conflict of interest and identity. It will also result in a crisis of faith.

Questions

1. *Can you think of examples of compromise which are testing the church today?*

2. *Are there things which come between you and God? What can you do about them?*

3. *What can we do to help Christians who are trapped in compromise and caught up in a crisis of faith?*

Geography

The neighbouring peoples (verse 1) More literally 'the peoples of the land', most of those groups mentioned were no longer nations as such.

The Canaanites, a semitic race, were decimated by Joshua's invasion of Canaan and by the time of Ezra were confined to the area around Tyre and Sidon. Earlier Canaanite city strongholds such as Beth-Shan and Megiddo had long ago passed into the hands of the Israelites: Solomon made Megiddo one of his chariot cities to ensure peace in the land (Jos.12:21; cf 1 Ki.9:15–19).

The Hittites mentioned here (not the Hittite nation of Asia Minor – modern day Turkey) were two tribal groups, one which lived in the south of Palestine and is mentioned in the Annals of Sargon II of Assyria. The people who lived in the Philistine city of Ashdod are called Hittites. The other resided in Syria and their king is referred to in 2 Chronicles 1:17. Uriah of the David and Bathsheba story was a Hittite soldier of fortune (2 Sa.11:3).

The Perizzites and Jebusites lived in the hill country near Bethel (Gn.13:7) and in the Judean hill country (Jdg.1:4f).

The Ammonites, according to Genesis 19:38, were descended from one of Lot's daughters and lived in an area between the Jabbok and Arnon rivers (Dt.2:20–21, 37; 3:11). They lost some of this territory later on to the 'Amorites'. The main city of the Ammonites was Rabbath Ammon (Amman today) where King Og's iron bed was (Dt.3:11). Israel captured the city in the time of David (2 Sa.12:26–31) and King Baalis of the Ammonites stirred up trouble for the Jews during the time of the Babylonian Empire (Je.40:11–14).

The Amorites, nomads and shepherds, were another of the peoples of Canaan (Gn.10:16) who originated from Syria. They were part of the reason for the demise of the Babylonian third dynasty when they took over a number of towns around Ur. One of its most famous kings is *Hammurabi* or *Hammurapi* whose law codes are contained on a 7ft. 4 in. stele which now resides in the Louvre in Paris.

The Moabites are sometimes called 'the sons of Seth' (Nu.24:17) and are descendants of Lot's other daughter (Gn.19:30f). Moab was famous in biblical times as the land of sheep and rams (2 Ki.3:4) and was east of the Dead Sea. The *Moabite Stone* has an inscription recording the victories of 'Mesha, king of Moab' over Israel in the ninth century BC. It was found at Diban (Dibon in Nu.21:30) and like Hammurabi's law codes, it can now be seen in the Louvre.

Biblical terms

Wives (verse 2) The word wife or wives does not actually appear in the Hebrew, the literal phrase used is *nasa*, – 'to lift up, to receive or take up' and is used again in verse 12 and 10:44. It is used in Ezra 5:15 in the context of taking vessels to the Temple. So where the NIV translates 'they have taken some of their daughters as wives' (verse 2) it could equally be translated as 'concubines' or 'cohabiters'. If the women taken were not wives but concubines it would make more sense of the situation described in chapter 10 because it was easier to get rid of a concubine than a wife (Gn.21:10–14), a situation which is reflected in the Babylonian law of King *Lipit Ishtar* number 25.

Fig.5: A traditional scribe at work

Ezra 9:8–15

The remaining Remnant

No matter what happens God will always make sure that there are those who will be saved.

After the initial shock of the news of the state of the nation Ezra embarks on a prayer which is a mixture of confession and intercession for God's people to return to a right relationship with him (verses 6–15).
There is mention of 'detestable practices' (verse 11). This is a direct reference to the list in Deuteronomy 18:9–12 involving witchcraft, divination and child sacrifices.

A new word makes its only appearance in Ezra in this chapter (verses 8,14,15) and once at the beginning of Nehemiah (Ne.1:2). The Hebrew word can be translated 'deliverance', 'escape', 'survive' or 'remainder'. It picks up an important piece of biblical theology which is echoed consistently throughout both the Old and New Testaments – that whatever else happens there will always be a righteous remnant who God will save from destruction.

When Lot was captured someone *escaped* to tell Abraham (Gn.14:13); Isaiah gives God's promise to King Hezekiah that a *remnant* of the house of Judah will survive (2 Ki.19:30-31) and the opening chapter of Nehemiah speaks of the *remnant* who have survived the exile in order to return to the promised land.

Another word for remnant is used in verse 13. It comes from the root word meaning 'remainder' or 'left over'. The meaning is 'remnant', 'survivor', 'those who escaped' (Gn.45:7; Ne.1:3; Is.10:21; 11:16; Zc.9:7). Both words for 'remnant' are used to express the same theological concept.

In the New Testament the Greek words used in Romans 9:27 and 11:5 have the same underlying meaning. The remnant are that group of people who have remained faithful to God and his covenant despite the surrounding pressures and problems of life. The promise of God that there will always be a remnant who remain in any given situation has the implication of judgment and hope: God will preserve. It is first made clear in the story of Noah (Gn.6:5; 9:12–17); Joseph's life is preserved by God (Gn.45:5); Elijah is reminded of the righteous remnant (1 Ki.19:18). Other examples include the holy stump cut off to grow again (Is.6:13), and the name of Isaiah's son *Shear Yashub*, means 'a remnant shall return'(Is.7:3).

Jesus becomes the remnant of one (Rom.5:12–21). Then the church with Christ as head becomes the remnant, 'Through the obedience of the one man the many will be made righteous' (Rom.6:19). That does not mean that everybody who belongs to a church will be included. Jesus himself made it clear that some would have a surprise when judgment day came (Mt.7:21; 25:31–46; Lk.6:46; 13:25). Those who do his will and try to live the life of faith will be the remaining remnant.

Questions

1. *Some people say that everybody will go to heaven in the end. What do you think?*

2. *Who is in a position to say they are part of the righteous remnant?*

3. *Why did God allow the Jews to be taken from their land in the first place?*

Biblical terms

A firm place (verse 8) The actual word used is 'tent peg' and implies somewhere where a tent can be securely pitched. There are also links with the tent of meeting, or Tabernacle, which was pitched with bronze tent pegs (Ex.27:19; 35:18; Nu.3:37).

The New Jewish Publication Society translates this, 'and given us a stake in His holy place'. So the Temple is seen as a safe place for the remnant.

A wall of protection (verse 9) Some have used this as an argument for Nehemiah coming before Ezra and his wall already being in place. But it is a metaphor and not intended to be taken literally, otherwise it would surround not only Jerusalem but the whole of Judah.

The nation Israel is often likened to a vineyard and it is more acceptable in the feel of this passage that the image of a wall is that surrounding a vineyard (Ps.80:12; Is.5:5) rather than a city wall.

Personnel

Through your servants the prophets (verse 11) It would be very easy to take this verse and assume it means the prophets in the technical sense (that is, the prophetic books), from Isaiah onwards. However, only one prophet speaks out specifically about intermarriage (verse 12) and that is Malachi (Mal.2: 11–12) and he was not around until after the second Temple was finished (Mal.3:1).

The phrase 'Servants the prophets' is actually a standard phrase meaning those who come from the tradition of prophets which began with Moses (Dt.18:15–18; 34:10; 2 Ki.17:13; 21:10; Je.7:25–26).

Ezra 10:1–4

Time to act

When people are really sorry for wrong-doing talk alone is not enough – actions speak louder than words.

Ezra's prayer in chapter 9 is a record of his own words. Here the account changes to the third person and reflects the fact that the events of both Ezra and Nehemiah are drawn from a number of sources.

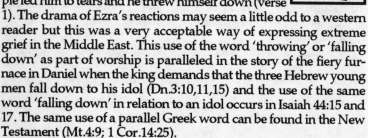

The results of Ezra's passionate prayer for the people led him to tears and he threw himself down (verse 1). The drama of Ezra's reactions may seem a little odd to a western reader but this was a very acceptable way of expressing extreme grief in the Middle East. This use of the word 'throwing' or 'falling down' as part of worship is paralleled in the story of the fiery furnace in Daniel when the king demands that the three Hebrew young men fall down to his idol (Dn.3:10,11,15) and the use of the same word 'falling down' in relation to an idol occurs in Isaiah 44:15 and 17. The same use of a parallel Greek word can be found in the New Testament (Mt.4:9; 1 Cor.14:25).

It is hardly unexpected that a large crowd gathered in response to Ezra's dramatic actions. His passion must have been powerful because it resulted in the men, women and children present weeping bitterly with him. Then Shecaniah, son of Jehiel, calls for practical action, it was time to act! 'Now let us make a covenant before our God...' (verse 3). There are two main words in Hebrew normally translated 'covenant', the one used here (verse 3) is *berith*, it can also mean 'treaty'. It is the only time it is used in Ezra and only occurs four times in Nehemiah (Ne.1:5; 9:8,32; 13:29).

The same word is used when God establishes his covenant with Noah (Gn.6:18), with Abraham (Gn.15:18), with Moses and the Israelites (Ex.19:5), and with King David and his descendants (2 Ch.13:5). The actual word normally associated with this idea is 'to cut a covenant', based on the religious rite of killing an animal and cutting it into two or three parts. Part of the animal was burnt as an offering and the part eaten in a religious meal sealed the covenant. This way of agreeing a covenant is found not only in the Bible (Gn.15:17; Ex.24:8; Je.34:18) but in a number of ancient Near Eastern texts including the *Mari texts* (a site on the west bank of the Euphrates river where 20,000 clay tablets were found) and the *Alalakh tablets* (found at Tel Atchana near the Turkish/Syrian border). Deuteronomy 29:9-14 refers to the cutting of a covenant involving women and children.

The blood of Jesus, which he refers to as the cup of the new covenant, is symbolized in wine (1 Cor.11:25). The Greek *diatheke* meaning 'covenant', 'testament' or 'will' (1 Cor.11:25) is used in speaking of the new relationship between God and those who believe through the sacrifice of his son.

The covenant is always initiated by God and Jesus reminds us of this:'You did not choose me, I chose you' (Jn.15:15). It is not a covenant between equals but rather like a treaty after a war, one strong and the other weak. A covenant with God is not a contract which you can opt out of by giving notice (Jos.9:3-15; 1 Sa.11:1f; 1 Ki.20:34). There are one or two instances of covenants with individuals but it is always with the wider community of God's people in mind (Je.32:36-40). The purpose of the covenant is mission (sending out the message of God) so that Israel is seen as a covenant for mission to the rest of the world (Is.49:8).

The call to action was a tough one: making a covenant entailed sending away all foreign women from Jewish households, and their children as well (verse 3). Sexual encounters with foreigners had always been forbidden and now those who had been disobedient were about to pay the price for their behaviour.

'Talk is cheap' and 'action speaks louder than words' are two popular sayings but with significant truths behind them. If I say to someone 'I love you', and then take no notice of that person what do the words prove? It is easy to say, 'I am a Christian', but what impression will that have on other people unless I practise what I preach? When things go wrong and life gets in a mess as a result of stupid behaviour and disobedience to God there is a time to confess wrong actions, a time to cry, but finally comes the point where it is time to act.

Questions

1. What do you think about men crying and why?

2. Do you feel it is right to break up families because of religion? Why?

3. How can the church act to show it means what it says?

Personalities

Shecaniah (verse 2) The difficulty of identifying the 'Shecaniah' here is that there appear to be five or six men with the same name, and the same is true of his father's name Jehiel.

What we do know is that he was a lay person from the Elam phratry (or clan within a tribe), many of whom made their return (*aliyah*) with the first group to arrive in Jerusalem (Ezr.2:7) and a few more with Ezra (Ezr.8:7); and he is mentioned again in Ezra 10:26.

He appears to be a leader of the people because of his willingness to follow Ezra's lead in confessing the guilt of the Jewish community. His lead produces an effective and positive response from the crowds gathered round.

Biblical terms

Foreign women (verse 2) The phrase in either the singular or plural recurs six times and only in chapter 10 of Ezra (verses 2, 10, 14, 17, 18, 44).

A number of prominent Old Testament men were married to foreign women including Esau who married two Hittites (Gn.26:34); Joseph who married an Egyptian (Gn.41:45); Moses who married a Midianite (Ex.2:21); David who married a Calebite and an Aramaean (2 Sa.3:3); and Solomon who married for wealth and to establish political treaties, Moabites, Ammonites, Edomites, Sidonians and Hittites (1 Ki.11:1; 14:21). These mixed marriages were of great concern because they took away from the Jewish purity of blood and were seen as a threat to religious faith (1 Ki.11:4). It was probably for these two main reasons that the practice was actually forbidden by Jewish law (Ex.34:15–16; Dt.7:3–4). The only exception seems to be those women captured in times of war as long as they abandoned their original nationality (Dt.21:10–14).

The problem was that many seemed to ignore these prohibitions when it suited them. It is borne out here (see Ne.10:30; 13:23–27; Mal.2:11–12).

Marrying (verse 2) The same word recurs in verses 10, 14, 17 and 18 and although translated 'to marry' actually literally means 'to sit down' or 'sit still'. Often translated 'to live', 'inhabit', 'endure', 'remain', 'stay', it can also mean, 'to cohabit'. It is only used in the sense of marriage here and in Nehemiah 13:23 and 27, although the actual word is used elsewhere in Ezra and Nehemiah in its more literal sense (Ezr.2:70; Ne.3:26; 4:12; 7:73; 8:14; 11:1–4,6,21 and 25; 13:16).

Normally a much stronger Hebrew word *baal* meaning 'to be master' or 'owner' is used to mean marriage (for example Ex.21:3; Dt.22:22; Is.54:1; Jer.3:14 and Mal.2:2).

Fig.6: Parading the Torah

Ezra 10:5–11

Make your mind up

The choice is always there, God's will or self-interest. Sometimes it's a tough choice.

The response of Ezra to Shecaniah's call to a new covenant was immediate. He was quick to seize the opportunity of the moment and ensure that this desire for a return to a right relationship with God was not lost in a cooling of passion. He called priests, leaders and people to make a public promise to put
their words into action. Oaths (verse 5) had the same courtroom imagery then as they do today (Nu.5:11–31; 1 Ki.8:31). It was seen as a religious test, but if a person refused to take the oath he was to be accepted as guilty and was linked to those who refused to be witnesses (Lv.5:1).

In Hebrew to 'take an oath' or to 'make a covenant' literally means 'to use a curse'. That is, 'if I break this vow may this curse come upon me' (1 Sa.14:24). Ezekiel 17:13–21 gives an account of an oath taken to seal a treaty (covenant) and the consequences of breaking it.

Jesus also took a very strong position on vows or oaths (Mt.5:33–37). As a result some religious groups today, such as the Society of Friends, will not take the oath of allegiance or courtroom oath. When

Jesus was asked, under oath, by the high priest, if he was the messiah he said, 'yes', but the high priest could not accept it, tore his clothes and accused him of blasphemy (Mt.26:63).

Just in case anybody had second thoughts Ezra had a proclamation sent to every area of Jerusalem and Judah (verse 7). It was definitely 'make your mind up' time! Anyone who failed to act according to the oaths taken by the gathering at the Temple would be excluded from 'the assembly of the exiles' (verse 8). Ezra gave the men (it was the men who had to make the decision in that culture) three days to gather in Jerusalem (verse 9).

Such was the impact on the nation that the book of Ezra records that by the deadline 'all the people were sitting in the square before the house of God' (verse 9). As if those who had cohabited with foreign women did not feel bad enough, now it began to rain. 'It never rains but when it pours'!

The word for rain (verse 9) used here and in verse 13 implies very heavy downpours rather than just the odd shower. The rainy season usually began mid to late October but might not start in earnest until the beginning of January. The final rains were normally over by the end of April, or the beginning of May. If Ezra's public reading is the one recorded in Nehemiah 8 the date is 20th of Kislev. This would be some time during the third week in December when it would not only be wet, but also very cold for the climate because it would be midwinter.

Rain downpours were used as an illustration of blessings being poured down on the kingdom by its king (Ps.72:6–7) or waiting for the coming of the messiah (Jas.5:7). I doubt the people in the square were feeling exactly blessed as they gathered there.

Have you ever noticed that most of the choices scripture puts before the Christian are tough ones? They are usually made worse because the call to 'come clean' is often the result of our own stupidity. Even if it is not the call to choose is no easier than that of the quizmaster who asks, 'Do you want to take the money or take a chance?'

The main difference is that even when the Christian feels he or she is under a cloud they can still be confident of the promise, '...in all things God works for the good of those who love him, who have been called according to his purpose' (Rom.8:28). The only condition is obedience and the call to make your mind up.

Questions

1. *Does your church tradition require you to make public promises, and if so, does it make it easier or harder for you to keep them?*

2. *If your church leadership make promises on your behalf are you prepared to back them by acting on those promises?*

3. *What do you think about non-Christians making promises in church buildings for the sake of a ceremony, but who obviously have no intention of keeping them?*

Personalities

Jehohanan (verse 6) The reference to Ezra visiting the house of Jehohanan, son of Eliashib, has been used as evidence that Nehemiah arrived in Jerusalem before Ezra. It is argued that Eliashib was high priest when Nehemiah first got to Jerusalem (Ne.3:1) and that in fact Eliashib's grandson Jehohanan, who inherited the priesthood (Ne.12:10–11), was high priest when Ezra reached Jerusalem.

Against this, the two names were very common during this period. Four different people called Eliashib and two different men named Jehohanan are mentioned just in Ezra 10, added to which the name in Nehemiah 12:11 is actually *Jonathan* and not *Jehohanan* which is quite different.

Biblical terms

Separate (verse 11) If the word 'cohabit' is used instead of 'marry' in verse 2 it would explain why the word 'separate' instead of 'divorce' is used in Ezra 10:11. There are two Hebrew words for 'divorce' (Lv.21:14; 22:13; Nu.30:9; Dt.24:1,3; Is.50:1; Je.3:8; Mal.2:16) and neither of them are used anywhere in either Ezra or Nehemiah in the context of relationships between men and women. They are also used to mean 'let', 'go' or 'send'. (for example, Ezr.4:11,14,17,18; 5:6–7; 6:12–13: 7:14; Ne.2:5,6,9; 4:4; 6:2–5, 8,12,19; 8:10,12).

The same word 'separate' is used elsewhere in Ezra and Nehemiah of breaking off relationships with those regarded as unclean (Ezr.6:21; 9:1; 10:8,11; Ne.9:2; 10:28; 13:3). It is also used of those who were set apart for a special purpose (Ezr.8:24; 10:16). This would be much more consistent with other Old Testament teaching where mixing with idol-worshipping peoples is regarded as a form of prostitution. Hosea accused Israel of 'playing the harlot' (Ho.2:5; 3:3; 4:12,14; 9:1). It then also explains why God's spokesperson, Ezra, should advocate separation to those cohabiting because marriage with those worshipping other gods was forbidden, and therefore probably not recognized.

Ezra 10:12–44

The great divorce

Life gets complicated when you go against God's will and it is harder to undo things than not to have done them in the first place.

The climax of the book of Ezra is quite tragic: the people responded to his call to separate themselves from the unbelievers, 'You are right! We must do as you say' (verse 12), but it was still a painful parting. A similar situation had occurred when Abraham tried to work out God's will for him and Sarah by taking her servant, Hagar, in order to produce a son. God did keep his promise and, against all the odds, Sarah produced a son, Isaac. Then Hagar and her son, Ishmael, were banished from the tribe (Gn.21:1–20).

'We have sinned greatly in this thing' (verse 13) – with a few notable exceptions the people accept Ezra's challenge and confess their guilt. 'We have sinned greatly' is the phrase used but the actual sin is implied rather than stated. Even in Ezra's dramatic outburst his concern is the fact that people were breaking the covenant (Ezr.9:10–12) and risking bringing down God's anger and judgment (Ezr.9:14). This is more than just getting rid of foreign women. It is about the purification and separation of God's people for his will and purpose (see verse 11) in order to avoid divine retribution.

'In this thing' – the word 'thing' is the Hebrew *dabar* usually translated 'matter', 'thing', 'word'. The basic root of the word is 'to speak' and the implication is God's word has been spoken. The power of God's word is reflected in Genesis 1 where God's word brought creation into being. 'The word of the LORD' is the voice of authority (Ezr.1:1). John picks this up when he makes it clear that Jesus is 'the Word...made flesh' (Jn.1:14 AV). In the Hebrew mind God's word and his activity are one and the same and not to be separated. His people are intended to be a reflection of this.

Divorce was not part of God's original intention for his people (Gn.2:24) and the only reason it was ever allowed was because of the hardness of the heart of Israel (Mt.19:8; Mk.10:5; cf Dt.24:1–4). Malachi makes it clear that God hates divorce but disobedience to the covenant is just as unacceptable (Mal.2:16). Like naughty children, those who don't conduct themselves in a godly way will always end up having to pay the price for disobedience. Even King David found this out to his cost (2 Sa.12:13–14).

The decision was a tough one for the nation of Israel but obedience was vital if they were to maintain their identity as God's covenant people. The alternative was to go the way of those who water down the will of God and lose their identity in him. The names of those who had been caught in compromise were posted for all to see in the same way that shopkeepers of the thirties depression in Britain put the names of bad debtors in their shop windows. The sad situation was resolved on 4th August (see Ezr.7:9). This meant that the whole unhappy business took about seventy-five working days to sort out a list of 119 cases.

Whenever the Church of Jesus Christ has tried to act other than in obedience to God's word it has declined to the point where it has become difficult to see where the ways of the world end and the position of the church begins. The Reformation became necessary because the church was no longer conducting itself according to the will of God and the great divorce of the church began. Since then many other denominations have arisen in an attempt to get back to the place where Jesus wants his people to be. Sadly, history demonstrates that each in turn has had to make the same journey as those Jews gathered at the Temple with Ezra – return, return to God's way or disappear.

The lesson to be learned is don't do it in the first place and then you don't have to endure the painful process of undoing it, disobeying Jesus' teachings only result in complications.

Questions

1. What examples of unholy alliances can you think of in the worldwide church today?

2. How far can we go as Christians in working alongside people who do not share our faith before we have to draw the line?

3. What is your reaction to churches who refuse to marry people who have been divorced?

Personnel

Elders and Judges (verse 14) 'Elders' are also mentioned in Ezra 5:5,9; 6:7,8,14, but not in Nehemiah. The particular word for 'elder' used only here and in verse 8, in Hebrew comes from the word 'beard' which in Ezra 9:3 is used of someone who is 'old', 'an elder', or 'chief magistrate'.

The elders had authority in civil affairs and assisted the chief priests in enforcing religious law amongst the clans identified with the towns and villages in Israel. They were also active during the exile (Ezk.8:1; 14:1; 20:1,3).

'Judges' – different Hebrew words are used in Ezra 4:9, and 7:25. The word used here is not found in this context anywhere else in Ezra or Nehemiah. The Hebrew word is used of someone who has the responsibility of 'governor' or 'magistrate', someone who 'decides' or 'defends'.

Persian judges and magistrates of the same period were called 'law bearers' and had the responsibility of advising on the law of the land but the final decision rested with the king. Darius was called 'the Law giver' by the peoples he ruled over. The Persians operated two kinds of court systems, one for dealing with family and property disputes, the other with taxation and crimes against the crown. In order to carry out this law scribes were used and it may be that Ezra carried out this legal state function as well as his religious role.

Times and seasons

First day of the tenth month (verse 16) It is esti-mated that this was 29th December 458 BC, ten days after Ezra's commission was established. The tenth month was *Tebeth* which was December/January, the time of rain and snow when sowing crops began.

Nehemiah 1:1–3

Dire straits

Freedom from captivity is not enough – it's what happens afterwards that counts.

Nehemiah was still working in Babylon when his brother, Hanani, brought the sad news from the home country about the state of Jerusalem. The problems on the surface were of a physical nature, but underlying everything else was the spiritual state of things. The people of God who had returned home in order to rebuild with so much enthusiasm had lost the vision. They were in dire straits; the big issue was why and what Nehemiah could do about the situation?

The same story has been repeated throughout the history of God's people. When folk have been close to God there has been a vision, an enthusiasm and energy to carry out his will and purpose. When the focus of life changes to personal desire, accumulation of wealth and legalism the spiritual temperature goes down to lukewarm. The result is apathy and a downward spiral into an eventual state of desperation which eventually turns individuals, churches, and nations back to God. The book of Judges is full of examples of this pattern. The sadness is that each generation normally fails to learn the lessons of its predecessors. So God's people have to relearn the lesson of need for God-centred lives, and the restoration of biblical values in order to restore love, justice, dignity and direction, first to the church, and then to society.

Nehemiah needed Hanani to tell him about Jerusalem. Paul wrote, 'how can they hear without someone preaching to them' (Rom.10:14) but would Paul have been used to tell people about Jesus if Barnabas had not gone to tell him about the need of the church at Antioch (Acts 11:25)? The great revival in the eighteenth century which some say prevented a revolution happening in Britain like the one in France began because someone told George Whitefield to go and preach to miners at Kingswood colliery near Bristol.

Paul told the crowd at Lystra that God never left himself without a witness to his love and concern for his creation (Acts 14:17). All who have discovered the saving power of Jesus are called upon to carry the message of good news, especially when the church is in dire straits.

Questions

1. Has God used someone to speak to you recently? If so, what was your experience?

2. Do you have a vision for God's will for your situation?

3. What has God set your church free from and why?

Personalities

Nehemiah (verse 1) The name means 'the Lord *(Yahweh)*has comforted'. This is an interesting comparison with his father's name, Hacaliah, which means either, 'the Lord is hidden' or, 'wait for the Lord'. Nehemiah is only mentioned in the Bible in the books of Ezra and Nehemiah but is also acknowl-edged in writings such as 2 Maccabees 1:18–36 in the Apocrypha, and Jesus Sirach 48:13 as one who played a major part in the Feast of Tabernacles and in the founding of a library. More than half this book is a personal diary of Nehemiah's experiences.

He was King Artaxerxes' cupbearer (see the note on verse 11) in 445 BC and later was appointed governor (2:11). He returned to Persia in 433 BC after the walls of Jerusalem had been rebuilt (5:14; 13:6). Nehemiah did come back to Jerusalem later on (13:7) but we cannot be certain of the date.

The Talmud[7] (a Jewish commentary on the Bible), says that Nehemiah had a short temper and was full of his own self-righteousness. This seems a little unkind, and we cannot be certain that it is true.

It is reasonable to make some assumptions based on the experiences of Daniel and his friends in Babylon. Nehemiah would probably be well-trained (Dn.1:4f) and most likely quite good-looking (Dn.1:4, 13, 15). He would need to know about wines, and being frequently in the presence of the king, was in a position of some influence (see the note on verse 11).

There are other uses of the name Nehemiah, (Ezr.2:2, Ne.3:16; 7:7) which should not be confused with Nehemiah the king's cupbearer.

Hanani (verse 2) He was probably Nehemiah's real brother although the word 'brother' was used sometimes just meaning 'a male relative'. Later he was appointed as Nehemiah's deputy and put in charge of the citadel at Jerusalem (7:2) which supports the belief that he was his brother.

His name means 'the Lord has been gracious' – another variation is Hananiah – and was quite a common name in the Old Testament. The name crops up on several lists in Ezra and Nehemiah (Ezr.10:28; Ne.3:8, 30; 10:23; 12:12, 41).

Times and seasons

The month of Kislev of the 20th year *Kislev or Chislev* is the ninth month in the Jewish calendar (November/December), the end of ploughing and the beginning of seed time.

'The twentieth year' of what is the question? Some scholars think this is a slip of the pen. They suggest it should really be the nineteenth year of the reign of Artaxerxes in order to account for Nehemiah 2:1. Here the month of Nisan is referred to as being in 'the twentieth year of King Artaxerxes'. Others suggest that it was the twentieth year since Hanani's departure but this is unlikely. Or it could be a reference to the twentieth year Nehemiah has spent at Susa but again this is unlikely because, as the king's cupbearer, he would move with the king.

If the year began in *Nisan* – the first month of the Babylonian calendar (see note on Ezr.7:8) the year in Nehemiah 2:1 would be the twenty-first year of King Artaxerxes. The question then must be, does Nehemiah regard *Tishri* as the first month – normally the seventh month (see Ezra 3:1)? The most acceptable argument is that the Jews calculated their calendar from the autumn and this would allow both months to be considered in the same year – 445 BC.[8]

Geography

The citadel of Susa Referred to by its Hebrew name *Shusan* in some versions, it was the spring residence of the Persian kings (about 150 miles north of the Persian Gulf) and one of the five capitals of the empire: the other four were Babylon, Parsagae, Persepolis and Ecbatana.

It was here that the events recorded in the book of Esther and the vision of Daniel took place (Dn.8:2). The law code *Stele of Hammurabi* was discovered at Susa. The site was first excavated by the archaeologist W.K. Loftus in AD 1851 and has since been taken over by the French (see the note on Ezra 4:9).

Nehemiah 1:4–11

Weep for the city

When we see things as God sees them then we can share his heart for the situation, and it usually leads to prayer.

The words of Hanani reached right down into Nehemiah's heart and brought him to tears (verse 4). This in turn led to mourning, fasting and deep, committed prayer. Then Nehemiah really began to share the father-heart of God for Jerusalem: a feeling which was now sharpening up into a vision of God's will which would drive Nehemiah into action.

Jesus wept over the city of Jerusalem as he shared his Father's heart (Lk.19:41), action followed as he first drove the money changers out of the Temple and led to his crucifixion. God's love went into action as Jesus died in my place and yours so that we could be rebuilt into the image of God.

When Salvation Army workers on the mission field felt they had come to a dead end and told the founder, William Booth, he sent back the message, 'try tears'.

Vision can only really be born out of sharing God's heart for a particular situation. Vision comes from being put in the picture to the point where your heart aches for something to be done about it.

Developing a real burden for that situation makes you cry out to God and drives you to prayer. Deep and committed, heartfelt prayer leads to the discovery of God's will and purpose – then it is time to act.

Too many people want Jesus to be their Saviour, to free them from their sins but stop there. Real growth with God means catching the vision for his will and purpose and then having the desire to do something about it.

Questions

1. *Have you ever wept before God in desperation over some thing or someone?*

2. *Why do you think Nehemiah wept, then mourned and fasted?*

3. *Should the church ask for God's help when it is not prepared to carry it out?*

Biblical terms

King's cupbearer (verse 11) The Hebrew verb used, literally means 'to give to drink'. So cupbearer means 'one who gives (someone) something to drink'. The same word occurs in 1 Kings 10:5 and 2 Chronicles 10:5. In some versions the phrase is translated 'but-ler' (Gn.40:1–23; 41:9). But the word 'butler' comes from an old English word meaning 'bottle attendant', and loses something of the meaning.

It was quite an important position of influence with direct access to the king, as we shall see. In the book of Tobit (the Apocrypha) the ruler Esarhaddon's cupbearer was said to be second only to the king (Tobit 1:22). The Greek historian, Herodotus records the story of King Cambyses appointing one of his friends' sons to the position of cupbearer as a great favour.[9]

The job of the cupbearer is described by Xenophon (c.430–354 BC), a pupil of Socrates, 'Now, it is a well-known fact that the cupbearers, when they proffer the cup, draw off some of it with a ladle, put it into their left hand, and swallow it down – so that, if they should put poison in, they may not profit by it'.[10]

Some have suggested that Nehemiah was also a eunuch because such a position probably brought him in contact with the king's harem. The fact that there is no reference to him having a wife or children is given as support for this argument.

It is certainly a possibility. However, it may also be connected with another issue. When the Old Testament was translated into Greek for the non-Hebrew-speaking Jews (called *the Septuagint* because it was done by seventy scholars) they made a mistake in translating the word 'cupbearer' in two versions *(Septuagint Codex Vaticanus* and *Septuagint Sinaiticus)*. The word should have been translated *oinochoos* but was actually translated *eunouchos* (eunuch). Only *Septuagint Codex Alexandrinus* got it right.

Also, the Hebrew word sometimes used for a eunuch is literally 'one who stands at the head of the king'. It is used twelve times in the book of Esther, seven times in the book of Daniel and never in Nehemiah. Even when it is used, it is normally intended to mean 'court official' rather than eunuch.

The same word is used of Haman (Est.7:8) and he is certainly not a eunuch, otherwise why did the king suspect him of trying to seduce the queen? As to the harem argument: laws on the harem show that, as long as certain codes of behaviour were observed, non-eunuchs could enter the harem.[11]

History
Fasting (verse 4)
See the comment on Ezra 8:21 (p. 88).

Nehemiah 2:1–9

The King's commission

Even when it seems impossible, the desire to carry out God's will and to respond to a vision given by him will open doors in most unexpected ways.

Nehemiah held an important position in the king's household so it was unlikely that he would release Nehemiah to respond to God's call to go to Jerusalem.

'I was very much afraid' (verse 2). There are probably two reasons for this statement: first it was a time of festivity (probably a drinking party; cf verse 1 and Est.1:3f) and, because Nehemiah looked miserable on such an occasion, he was risking the king's anger. Secondly, he knew that the king had given orders for building work at Jerusalem to be stopped (Ezr.4:8–23). So how was the king going to react to the request Nehemiah was about to put to him? Notice Nehemiah does not actually name Jerusalem (2:5).

If the king felt that Nehemiah was involved in some plot against him then his life was at stake. Kings in those days were often quite paranoic, and with good reason. Many were killed by those who were close to them.

122

Nehemiah needed the king's permission to carry out the King's commission, but how? He never seemed to lose the proper perspective on his situation. When the king asked him what he wanted Nehemiah's number one priority was prayer (verse 5).

He may well have remembered the task given by God to Moses to go back to Egypt where Moses was in trouble for murder, and ask one of the most powerful rulers of the time to let a large proportion of his slaves (who were carrying out his building programme free of charge!) go free.

An impossible task, yet the Hebrew nation was released and after forty years in the wilderness made it into the land just as God had promised them. (Most of this story is found in the book of Exodus through to the book of Judges.)

Jesus dealt with a seemingly impossible situation with his disciples. While he was up the Mount of Transfiguration some of the disciples had tried to help a young boy who was possessed by a spirit.

When Jesus returned and the father asked him if he could help Jesus' response was, 'If you can? ... Everything is possible for him who believes' (Mk.9:23). Then he restored the lad to full health.

Afterwards the disciples asked him why they had failed and received the answer, 'This kind can come out only by prayer' (Mk.9:14–29).

Throughout the history of the church those people regarded as people of vision have also been people of prayer. They lived by the conviction that the task ahead was nothing compared to the power behind them.

Nehemiah was about to begin a journey both physically and spiritually. He was only just beginning to experience the power of prayer and what it means to serve the God of the impossible.

Nothing significant has changed; God is still calling people of prayer and vision to rebuild a fallen world and a damaged society.

To misquote the late president of the United States, J.F. Kennedy, 'Ask not what God can do for you, but rather what can you do for God'.

Our calling is to serve the God of the impossible and carry out the King's Commission.

Questions

1. *Can you think of times in your life when prayer has changed things? How?*

2. *Does your church believe in miracles?*

3. *How many times do people say it cannot be done with the result that nothing happens?*

Times and seasons

The month of Nisan in the 20th year (verse 1)
See the note on Nehemiah 1:1

Biblical terms

The queen sitting beside him (verse 6) It is odd that this phrase is included for no apparent reason. We know from Persian texts that Artaxerxes' queen was called Damaspia (*Persika* 15:44). However, the queen is not named here and the word translated 'queen' is not the usual one, *hammalkah,* but a much less popular word, *hassegal.*

It is a word usually used of 'a concubine' or 'woman of the harem' (Jdg.5:30; Ps.45:10; Dn.5:2–3, 23). Whoever she was, she was important enough for Nehemiah to mention. It suggests that she may have had a hand in persuading the king to go along with Nehemiah's request.

History

Governors of the Trans-Euphrates (verse 7) The word for 'governor' is also sometimes translated 'satrap' (see the notes on Ezra 4:10 and 8:36).

Personalities

Asaph (verse 8) He was the warden of the forests to
the king. The forests are probably those in Lebanon
that had supplied the wood for the building of the
Temple of Solomon (see the note on Ezr.2:7).

His name is Jewish in origin (which may be why
Nehemiah knew him by name). Another Asaph, not
to be confused with him, is mentioned as the lead singer in the
Temple choir in the time of King David (1 Ch.16:4–5).

Fig. 7: The king's cupbearer

Nehemiah 2:10–16

Know the worst

To achieve the best for God it is important to be realistic and to know the worst in a situation first.

It is interesting to observe how Nehemiah went about carrying out the King's commission once he had arrived in Jerusalem.

He did not charge straight in with a lot of fuss and commotion. He did not instantly proclaim himself as God's answer to all the troubles of the people of God. Instead he kept quiet until he had a full grasp of the situation. The enemy, Sanballat and Tobiah, had already got wind of Nehemiah's presence and it would not do to face them unprepared.

Sanballat the Horonite (verse 10) is mentioned not only in scripture but also in the Elephantine papyri (letters from Jews in Elephantine, Egypt) where he is known as the governor of Samaria, and where reference is also made to his two sons. His name is Babylonian and means 'the god Sin has given life'.[12] This is supported by Nehemiah 4:2 where Sanballat has an army and 6:2–5 where he summons Nehemiah as an equal.

In a letter (407 BC) to Bagoas, the governor of Judah[13], his sons are named as Delaiah and Shemaiah. Both names are based on the name of God, *Yahweh*, so he may well have worshipped the God of Israel. One of his daughters was married to Joiada, son of Eliashib the high priest (Ne.13:28).

The fact that he is called a Horonite implies that he came from the town of Horonaim. That could be a place in Moab (Je.48:3) or the village of Beth-Horon 18 miles north-west of Jerusalem. Sanballat was probably the descendant of one of the foreign families who settled there in the eighth century (2 Ki.17:24).

Tobiah (verse 10) has a Hebrew name meaning 'the Lord is good'. He obviously has strong ties with priestly Jewish families (6:17-19; 13:4). The name Tobiah was a well-known name in Moab at the later time of Greek influence. The name is also linked with the Jerusalem priesthood[14] so it may be that they were descendants of this Tobiah.

It is strange therefore, that he is described as an Ammonite. Unless it means simply that he was the Persian-appointed governor of the region because he is of equal status with Sanballat. Ammonites were completely excluded from the assemblies of Israel (13:1; see the note on Ezr.9:1).

Nehemiah realized that he would have to know the worst about the situation before he could begin to work for God's best. It was no use being so heavenly minded that he was of no earthly use! So, quietly by night, he set out to assess the state of the city walls. Nehemiah, the night-rider, found the walls in such a bad state that he was forced to dismount from his animal, but at least now he could make a realistic evaluation of the task to be achieved. Still he had told no-one (verse 16).

Jesus warned about the hypocrites (religious leaders) who liked to shout about their good works; he implies that their only real interest was to blow their own trumpets. The context was the Sermon on the Mount on the subject of service, prayer and fasting (Mt.6:1-18).

When God calls believers to carry out the work of the kingdom it is not for us to seek personal gratification. Nor should we charge in without knowing the full facts, like a child running full tilt down a hill-side out of control. Jesus knew the worst (the cross) but then achieved God's best (victory over sin and death). The message of Nehemiah has not changed – know the worst then you can work for the best.

Questions

1. *Do you ever say something and then wish you had thought about it first? How do you control your tongue?*

2. *Are there situations where the church duplicates work already being done because no-one bothered to ask first?*

3. *What is the worst and best in God's call on your life?*

Geography

Landmarks of the city (verses 13–15) (see the map of Jerusalem). This is one of the best descriptions of the city of Jerusalem during this period that we have on record. There are some difficulties in working out exactly where all the places mentioned are located. This is because the precise line followed by the city walls changed from one period to the next. Some gates named here cannot be found and probably disappeared during King Herod's rebuilding in the city. Interestingly, the archaeologist Kathleen M. Kenyon when discussing Nehemiah's description of the city walls says, 'The archaeological evidence therefore fits the literary evidence very well'[15].

The Valley Gate (verse 13) is said to be about 1,500 yards from **the Dung Gate**, where the rubbish was removed from the city (still there today), on the western wall. It led to the *Tyropeon* or 'Cheesemakers Valley' and could well be the 'Potsherd Gate' of Jeremiah 19:2.

The Jackal's Well (verse 13) is sometimes called the 'Dragon's well'. It is thought to be the 'Fuller's Spring' of En-rogel. It is now known as 'Job's Well' and is about 250 yards south of the southern tip of the city wall. It was close to the 'Serpent's Stone', a well-known landmark of the time (1 Ki.1:9).

The Fountain Gate (verse 14) was probably near the south-east corner of the city wall leading to En-rogel in the Kidron Valley.

The King's pool (verse 14) is probably the 'Pool of Siloam' (3:15 cf Jn.9:7) near to the 'Fountain Gate', a basin fed by the 'Gihon Spring'. It still exists and is known today as Birket el Hamra. When she excavated this part of the city Kathleen Kenyon wrote: 'The tumble-down stones uncovered by our trench is a vivid example of the ruinous state of the eastern side of Jerusalem that balked Nehemiah's donkey'.[16]

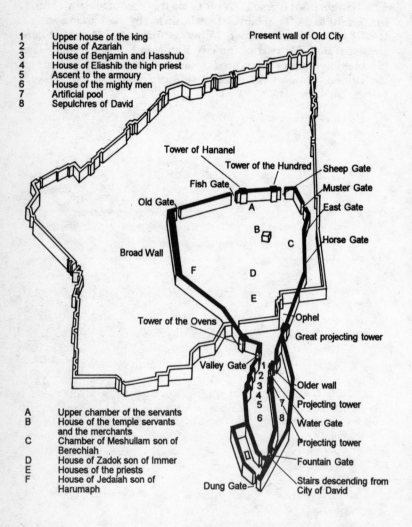

1 Upper house of the king
2 House of Azariah
3 House of Benjamin and Hasshub
4 House of Eliashib the high priest
5 Ascent to the armoury
6 House of the mighty men
7 Artificial pool
8 Sepulchres of David

Present wall of Old City

Tower of Hananel

Tower of the Hundred

Sheep Gate

Fish Gate

Muster Gate

Old Gate

East Gate

Broad Wall

Horse Gate

Tower of the Ovens

Ophel

Great projecting tower

Valley Gate

Older wall

Projecting tower

Water Gate

Projecting tower

Fountain Gate

Stairs descending from City of David

Dung Gate

A Upper chamber of the servants
B House of the temple servants and the merchants
C Chamber of Meshullam son of Berechiah
D House of Zadok son of Immer
E Houses of the priests
F House of Jedaiah son of Harumaph

Map 2: Jerusalem in Nehemiah's time

Nehemiah 2:17–18

One for all and all for one

People working together for the kingdom achieve far more than those who just want to do their own thing.

The foundations for the task had been laid in prayer, fasting, and vision. Then came the commission, determination and investigation. Now Nehemiah called the Jewish people to work together to rebuild the walls of the city. He called for co-operation to restore the honour of God and informed them of the goodwill of King Artaxerxes towards the task.

The word 'hand', symbolic of power and strength, is used in two different ways in these couple of verses. First Nehemiah claims God's authority by saying, 'the gracious hand of my God upon me'. Then the Jews respond by 'making their hands strong for the work' (see the note on verse 18). It could almost be paraphrased, 'Many hands make light work, especially when God is giving a hand'.

Nehemiah could not rebuild on his own; it was important that all the people of God played their part.

A rowing boat needs all hands on the oars. Too many passengers and it gets nowhere fast. Too much one-sided rowing and it goes round in circles. To be fast and effective everyone needs to give a hand.

There is no room for passengers in the work of the kingdom of God. Jesus, using the imagery of harvest-time, remarked to his disciples that the work needs to be done, but the workers are few (Mt.9:37; Lk.10:2).

The motto of the Three Musketeers in Alexander Dumas' novel of the same name should also be the motto of the Church of Jesus Christ, 'One for all and all for one' if we are to see the kingdom come, God's will done and his name given due honour.

Questions

1. What is the task God is calling you to co-operate in?

2. Can you achieve more on your own or working with others? Why?

3. Why do some churches insist on doing their own thing regardless of other Christians in the area?

Biblical terms

In disgrace (verse 17) More literally the Hebrew word is translated 'to shame', or 'reproach', from the root word meaning 'to strip' or 'pluck off'.

Although translated differently (Ne.4:4; 5:9; 6:13) all use the same word and the implication is that of losing face and being left with a bad name or reputation.

So they began this good work (verse 18) It is not entirely clear why the NIV translates the text here in this way. The actual Hebrew text is 'so they made their hands strong for good'. This is a Hebrew phrase meaning that they were encouraged.

The word translated as 'discourage' in Ezra 4:4 literally means 'weakened their hands' and was a well-known idiom of the time. What we have here in verse 18 is the opposite, that is, 'they were encouraged by (his) co-operation', which is different in its emphasis.

Fig. 8: Israelite labourers
(Taken from a marble relief in Sennacherib, king of Assyria's palace)

Nehemiah 2:19–20

Who is on the Lord's side ?

Partnership in God's purposes needs to be clearly defined – it only takes one bad apple to spoil the rest.

Nehemiah had gained the confidence of the people gathered in Jerusalem and now there was an air of real excitement and enthusiasm to begin rebuilding the walls. However, when God is at work with his people then the Devil, or his representatives, will usually be on hand to try and make things difficult.

Geshem (verse 19) was the third enemy of Nehemiah to be mentioned by name. He is also called *Gashmu* (6:6) in some translations. He is described as *Geshem the Arab* and there is evidence to show that he may well have been from a north Arabian tribe called the *Kedarites*. They crop up quite frequently in the Old Testament (Gn.25:13; 1 Ch.1:29; Is.21:16–17; 42:11; 60:7; Je.2:10; 49:28–33; Ezk.27:21). By the time of Nehemiah they had settled in the Transjordan area and down to the Nile Delta.

It has been suggested that one reason for Geshem's opposition to the new Jewish governor, Nehemiah, was that this strengthened province might interfere with trade. The powerful north Arabian confederacy controlled an area from north-east Egypt to northern

Arabia and southern Palestine. It gained much wealth from the myrrh and frankincense business.[17]

A bowl was discovered in 1947 at Tell el-Maskhuata in Egypt with the inscription 'Cain son of Gashmu king of Kedar' on it. This is almost certainly a reference to the same Geshem.

Sanballat, Tobiah and Geshem represented the surrounding nations and saw this conviction and unity among the Jews as a real threat to their own interests and power; something had to be done to stop it.

The first move was to attempt to lower the morale of the workers, and break their spirit before things went too far. Mockery, false accusations and ridicule are the stock in trade of opponents of God. Nehemiah's response was immediate; you have no legal, political or religious claim on this work (verse 20).

When Jesus began his public ministry, immediately he was baptized and the Holy Spirit came down, Satan was waiting for him in the wilderness to tempt him away from his work.

The devil tried to get at Jesus by appealing to his material needs, a call to compromise his commission and loyalties and temptation to outright sensationalism. Jesus consistently countered Satan's remarks with God's word – 'it is written' (Mt.4:1–11).

Self-interest and a desire for power are often the reasons Christians meet opposition when living out their lives according to God's will. So it is important to face attacks straight away and deal with them in a godly and biblical manner.

If you have a bad apple in a fruit bowl the longer you leave it there the more fruit it will infect. It is best to take it out immediately and avoid further problems.

If you ignore problems they do not go away, they just get bigger. When you are under any form of attack, be it ridicule or false accusations, recognize the enemy as well as your allies. Know who is on the Lord's side and act accordingly.

Questions

1. If people laugh at you and say untrue things about you because of your beliefs, how do you handle it?

2. What would your church do if someone came along to your church service and began to heckle the preacher?

3. Where do you draw the line in working in co-operation with people of other faiths or no faith at all?

Biblical terms

no share...claim or historic right (verse 20). The language used at this point comes from a law of the time that denied a 'share' through *political* dissocia- tion (2 Sa.20:1; 1 Ki.12:16). 'Claim' refers specifically to *legal* rights. 'Historic right' or traditional right probably means *religious* right through a memorial (Jos.4:7; Zc.6:14). In other words, Nehemiah is making it clear that he will not be involved with them in any way at all (compare Ezr.4:2).

The God of heaven (verse 20)
(see note on Ezra 1:2).

Nehemiah 3:1-32

Equal opportunities

God has a part for everyone to play in his purposes, often those who in the eyes of the world do not appear exactly suitable.

Work on the walls begins and this chapter gives us a record of who did what, where and with whom.

The use of language suggests that the north wall was completely destroyed because it was *rebuilt* whereas other parts were *re-enforced*.

Of the repairs carried out on the walls by the priests, Levites, gatekeepers, tradespeople, women, craftsmen (including goldsmiths and perfume makers) and officials forty-one separate repairs are listed. The phrase 'next to' which is used again and again in this passage literally means 'hand by hand'. It repeats the emphasis of 'many hands making light work' in chapter 2.

The northern section had eight task groups (verses 1-5), the west had ten (verses 6-13), the south had two (verses 14-15) and the east had twenty-one (verses 16-32) because a new wall had to be built here. It was also here that Nehemiah had to dismount from his donkey (2-14).

Shallum's daughters worked alongside the men (verse 12) and a whole town worked together to repair 500 yards of wall (verse 13).

But what about the leaders from Tekoa? The folk from Tekoa did not get into any arguments, they simply did twice as much work to cover for their leaders (verses 5 and 27).

If I was going to rebuild and restore a city wall I would probably have called in a professional building company. Nehemiah called together ordinary people, perfume makers and goldsmiths, men and women alike.

What is even more significant is that the work was completed in fifty-two days (6:15) and was good enough to walk on (12:31).

The Jews of Jerusalem and the surrounding areas had been called, commissioned and were about to prove they were also capable of carrying out the work.

There is an old hymn which begins, 'God works in a mysterious way his wonders to perform', and this is borne out in the account of the wall repairs.

If I had been in Jesus' position when he was looking for disciples I would have gone to Jerusalem Bible College, or the equivalent, for students who came highly recommended by the principal.

Jesus went to the north-west of the country and selected Galileans. Galilee was an area known for its thick northern accent and rebellious people. In Jerusalem they were regarded as being 'a bit thick' but they knew they had been with Jesus (Acts 4:13). It may not make a lot of sense in respect of the world's values but it makes perfect sense in terms of the values of the kingdom of God.

Later in history Paul would write to Greek Christians in Corinth who prided themselves on their intellect, 'Not many of you were wise by human standards; not many were influential; not many were of noble birth. But God chose the foolish things of the world to shame the wise; God chose the weak things of the world to shame the strong' (1 Cor.1:26–27).

The message of Nehemiah, Jesus and Paul is consistently the same. God has a special job for each one of us and the main qualification is a willingness to respond to his call. God is a real equal opportunities employer.

Questions

1. What qualifications do we need to do God's work?

2. What lessons can Christians today learn from the cooperation that took place to achieve God's will?

3. What would you do if some of your leaders refused to get involved in something that you felt was of God?

Geography
Landmarks of the city (verses 1–32)

In this section we have the opportunity to expand our knowledge of Jerusalem at the time of Nehemiah, following on from chapter 2:13–15. The challenge is to identify places where the names have significantly changed since (see Map 2 on p. 130).

The Sheep Gate (verse 1) was built on the eastern part of the north wall, facing the road to Jericho, by the high priest and his family (see also Jn.5:2). It could have been the site of a sheep market much the same as the one held outside *Herod's Gate* in the Old City in Jerusalem today. Some scholars identify it with the *Benjamin Gate* (Je.37:13; 38:7; Zc.14:10).

The Hundred's Tower (verse 1) could well mean it was the head-quarters of a garrison of 100 men similar to the Roman centurion structure. Compare 2 Samuel 18:1 where David set men over thousands and hundreds.

The Tower of Hananel (verse 1) was the most northern point of the wall where it turned south (2 Ch.33:14). It is also mentioned in 12:39 and Jeremiah 31:38 and could be part of a fortress. The historian Josephus mentions the fortress of Herod.[18] It is basically in the same location, and was probably the fortress in the Nehemiah period referred to as the Temple citadel or fortress (Ne.2:8).

The Fish Gate (verse 3) Just like the Sheep Gate, this may have been the site of a fish market (Ne.13:16) especially as it was on the western side of the city closest to the sea. Other names in the same geographical area are the *Ephraim Gate* (8:16; 12:39; 2 Ki.14:13) and

139

the *Middle Gate* (Je.39:3).

The Jeshanah Gate (verse 6) The name can be translated as 'the Gate of the Old City or Wall', it is uncertain which. This could have been a part of the original western wall. The other possibility is that it is associated with the village of Jeshanah (2 Ch.13:19) about fifteen miles north of Jerusalem but then it would have to be situated on the north wall in order to face Jeshanah just as the *Damascus Gate* of modern Jerusalem points towards Damascus. The difficulty with that view is that there does not appear to be room for it in Nehemiah's outline.

The Broad Wall (verse 8) lay between the *Ephraim Gate* and the *Tower of Ovens* (12:38f). The possibility is that it was a wall intended to cross the dip between the *City of David* and the *Temple Mount* because it branches off from the main wall and joins it again by the *Pool of Siloam*.

N. Avigad rediscovered 440 metres of this wall while excavating the Jewish quarter of the city in AD 1970–71 . It was found to be seven metres thick.

The Tower of Ovens (verse 11) is likely to have been the bakers' ovens. They were located south of the *Broad Wall* (12:38). Jeremiah speaks of the *Bakers' Street* that may be connected (Je.37:21).

The Valley Gate, the Dung Gate, the Fountain Gate, the Pool of Siloam (verses 13–14) see *Landmarks of the City* (Ne.2:13–15).

The Kings Garden (verse 15) is thought to be placed at the southern end of the *Kidron Valley* (2 Ki.25:4).

The City of David is used here to mean a smaller part of Jerusalem. This was on the south-eastern hill of the main city and to the north-west of the Gihon Spring. It was the original Jebusite town that David captured, sometimes called *Zion* (2 Sa.5:7), and covered an area of about fifteen acres. The city had the Tyropeon valley to its western side, the Hinnom valley was to the south, and the Kidron valley to the east. Solomon enlarged it to the north taking in the Temple mound (1 Ki.3:1; 11:27).

The graves of David (verse 16) have yet to be discovered but are thought to be near the King's Garden. David himself was buried in the City of David (1 Ki.2:10), the other graves are presumably those of members of his family (1 Ki.11:43).

The artificial pool (verse 16) translates literally as 'the pool that is made (by men)'. It may be the *Lower Pool* of Isaiah 22:9.

The House of Heroes (verse 16) is most probably an army barracks connected with 'the heroes of David' (2 Sa.16:6; 23:8f).

The armoury (verse 19) was apparently in the City of David, and 'the angle' was probably a significant change of direction of the wall.

Eliashib's house (verse 20) was south of the Temple, some distance away for the high priest's house. Maybe he did not want to be too close to his work!

Azariah's house (verse 23) was another private house mentioned as a landmark and suggests that Nehemiah was not consistently following the line of the old city walls. This is consistent with archaeological examination of the area, although some houses were built into city walls (Jos.2:15).

The court of the guard (verse 25) is also mentioned in Jeremiah 32:2. Normally translated 'guard' or 'guardhouse' the word can also mean 'prison' or 'place where people are watched'.

The Water Gate (verse 26) was located close to the Gihon Spring. Kathleen Kenyon, the archaeologist claimed to have found the northern tower of this gate in her excavations of Jerusalem.[19] There was a large square in front of it that was used for public assemblies (Ne.8:1).

The great projecting tower (verse 27) was obviously a well-known feature of that time but nothing more is known about it.

The wall of the Ophel (verse 27) The name means 'swelling'. The hill of Ophel was the beginning of the Temple hill going up the north end of the eastern ridge of the city. The wall itself may have been the outer wall of the area mentioned in 2 Chronicles 33:14. It was originally the northern defence wall of the *City of David* (2 Ch.27:3).

Kathleen Kenyon describes her excavation of Nehemiah's wall at this point as, 'solidly built, c.2.75 metres thick, but its finish was rough, as might be expected in work executed so rapidly'.[20]

The Horse Gate (verse 28) It is also mentioned in 2 Ki.11:16 and 2 Ch.23:15 where it is placed somewhere between the palace and the Temple near the priests' quarters. Jeremiah 31:40 describes it as a city gate as here; it was probably one of the main routes of the city.

Zadok's house (verse 29) Zadok ben-Immer was a priest (Ezr.2:37; Ne.10:21) and his next-door neighbour, Shemaiah, was a gatekeeper (10:28, 11:19).

The East Gate (verse 29) was one of the Temple gates (Ezk.40:6f).
The house of temple servants (verse 31) would be their accommodation, by the east wall opposite the Temple, rather than their home.
The Inspection (Muster) Gate (verse 31) could be identified with the *Gate of the Guard* (12:39) and the *Gate of the Appointed Place* (Ezk.43:21). This was the place where the sin offering was made.

Nehemiah 4:1–3

Angry opposition

The people of God can expect opposition from others when they carry out God's will – mockery is a favourite method of the ungodly, followed by anger.

Sanballat had tried to prevent the work from starting and had failed. Now the work was in progress it was no longer an idea to be laughed at but there was a real possibility, even probability, that the wall would be reconstructed and Sanballat was angry! The Hebrew word used implies 'being heated' or 'on fire'.

As is often the case he had his cronies with him, as well as the army of Samaria. The threat to Nehemiah had moved from words to a real physical threat in this show of force.

Sanballat questions the ability of the Jews to rebuild the walls but, despite mocking them in front of his friends and allies, he was obviously taking them seriously.

Tobiah adds fuel to the fire when he implies the wall would not even hold the weight of a fox walking on it (verse 3). According to Oscar Wilde, 'Sarcasm is the lowest form of wit and the highest form of ignorance'. It certainly did not stop the work from continuing.

It is rare for the work of God's people to go unopposed. If you love God it is highly likely that those who do not share your convictions will not love you (Jn.15:19–21).

Jesus was and is the most perfect person who has ever lived and yet even he had his critics. He was subjected to similar taunts and physical threats to Nehemiah and yet he was not defeated. Despite everything the opposition could throw at him Jesus completed the work his father sent him to do with the cry, 'It is finished' (Jn.19:30).

It should come to us as no surprise when we meet the same kind of reaction. Jesus warned his disciples that opposition and persecution would come and offered hope through perseverance: 'Blessed are you when people insult you, persecute you and falsely say all kinds of evil against you because of me' (Mt.5:11).

Questions

1. *How do you feel and react when you are criticized?*

2. *Do you know of churches where people have been threatened physically because they were Christians?*

3. *What do you think Jesus meant when he said we are blessed when we are persecuted for him?*

Biblical terms

Feeble Jews (verse 2) The word 'feeble', sometimes translated 'miserable', comes from a Hebrew root word used of a 'withering plant' drying up (for example: Is.16:8; 33:9; Je.14:2; La.2:8; Ho.4:3). So it suggests a person with no staying power whose efforts will all dry up into nothing. It also hints at lack of masculinity.

Foxes (verse 3) were inclined to be found in ruins (Ps.63:10; La.5:18; Ezk.13:4; translated as 'Jackal' in the NIV). The same Hebrew word *shual* translates into 'fox' and 'jackal'. Foxes were sometimes confused with jackals which look very similar, which is possibly why the same Hebrew word is used of both, so that only the context of the passage makes it clear which is meant.

Nehemiah 4:4–6

Prayer changes things

Prayer under pressure can be because of the desire for revenge but retribution is for God to decide, not us.

Nehemiah always turns to prayer in crucial situations and this one was no exception. The prayer appears to be a harsh one when we read it today in a different cultural setting. Why did Nehemiah pray in the way that he did?

Psalm 137 (made famous by the singing group 'Boney M'), begins by expressing a feeling of isolation a long way from home. The psalm moves from a feeling of sadness to anger at being in captivity. It ends with a prayer of bitterness asking God to smash the heads of the babies of their enemies against the rocks. Hardly a prayer of love and compassion!

Similar prayers can be found in Psalms 7, 35, 58, 59, 69, 83, 109, 137, 139. They may appear more than a little uncharitable to us today. However, in Nehemiah's mind would be the thought that this was God's work and so those who were opposing him were against God.

It is not a personal desire for punishment, which is put into God's hands. The covenant of Abraham included curses on the enemies of Israel (Gn.12:1–3) and supports Nehemiah's concern that no-one should sneer at the work of God.

Having 'got it out of his system' Nehemiah returns to the task in hand, rebuilding the wall. He has the same kind of determination which Jesus reflected when he commented, 'Destroy this temple, and I will raise it again in three days' (Jn.2:19).

There are occasions when we can feel so frustrated by evil actions that we are tempted to take the law into our own hands. However, it is for God to act as judge, not you or me and this is clearly stated in Deuteronomy 32:35 (quoted in Rom.12:19 and Heb.10:30).

Human nature seems to have an in-built desire to want to have a say in what goes on, to act as judge and jury on the lives of others.

Peter wanted to know what Jesus had to say about John and was told in so many words, by Jesus, to mind his own business (Jn.21:23).

Minding my own business means getting on with the job God has called me to do. The only way I am free to comment on other people's lives is in prayer.

Like Nehemiah, it is our responsibility to take it to the Lord in prayer, knowing that it is prayer which ultimately changes things. Then it is back to work.

Questions

1. Can you pray for Satan to be saved? If your answer is 'no' do you think you could prove it with a biblical answer?

2. Jesus says to love your enemies (Mt.5:44) but is it easier said than done? How can we love our enemies?

3. Does your church pray about people they do not like, or who make them angry and upset? How does it respond to people who oppose anything Christian with anything from ridicule to downright persecution?

Weights and measures

Half its height (verse 6) By now the wall was redefined around the city and half completed. Half its height in the Hebrew is 'up to its half' or 'to its middle'. Some scholars have suggested that this could mean the width, or even the length, but the height is consistent with Tobiah's comments.

Nehemiah 4:7–9

Watch and pray

Prayer is one aspect of spiritual warfare against an enemy, another is being constantly ready for attacks.

They were surrounded: the men of Ashdod to the west; Samaritans led by Sanballat to the north; Tobiah and the Ammonites to the east; and the Arabs, including the Edomites, led by Geshem to the south. It was rather like the feeling the Jews have in Israel today! It also gives some insight into the problems of a central government trying to maintain order from a distance. Persia was a long way away (see Map 3).

The leaders of the surrounding areas continued to do everything they could to prevent the work being completed. Nehemiah's strategy against them followed similar lines to those of Jesus when he said, 'Watch and pray' (Mt.26:41; Mk.14:38; Lk.21:36), stressing the necessity of being constantly on guard against attack.

There is a story told of the evangelist Dwight L. Moody coming by ship to conduct a mission in Britain. One of his followers informed him that the ship was on fire and enquired as to whether they should pray about it. 'Ay lad, as we're passing the fire buckets', came the reply.

The kingdom of God is a partnership between God and his people, each playing a responsible part. God helps those who help themselves and the call is consistently the same. Be practical in your spirituality, constantly before God in prayer and at the same time ready for anything. Watch and pray.

Questions

1. Is it reasonable to expect God to help us when we are not prepared to do anything ourselves?

2. What kind of attacks does your church have to be on guard against?

3. Who do you think are the enemies of the church?

Biblical terms

The repairs (verse 7) The Hebrew word used here is not the usual one used for 'repair' in Nehemiah. Taken literally the word means 'the healing (of an injury)' or 'health', 'recovery', 'restoration' (Je.8:22; 30:17; 33:6).

The more usual word for 'repair' is *chazaq*. This means 'to grow firm or strong' (Ne.3:4–12, 16–18, 22–23, 28–32).

Geography

Men of Ashdod (verse 7) They came from the coast area to the west of Jerusalem that had been the land of the Philistines.

Ashdod was the name of one of the five main Philistine cities. It was sacked by King Sargon II of Assyria in 720 BC when the people from there rebelled against him (Is.20:1; Amos 1:8). Ashdod gave its name to the whole of Philistia except Ashkelon that now was part of Tyre, and Gaza that stayed independent.

After the Babylonian Empire was established, Ashdod was made a province but was practically deserted (Zp.2:4; Zc.9:6) until it was partly reoccupied after the exile (Ne.13:23-24).

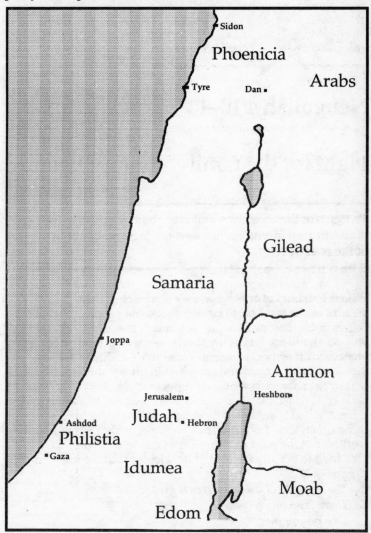

Map 3: Israel and the surrounding nations

Nehemiah 4:10–14

Fight for the family

To fight for those you love and care about the most in life is one of the greatest incentives to overcome fear and doubt in the face of the enemy.

With the amount of opposition they were facing and the size of the task still to be completed the people began to be discouraged. In very much the same way as the black slaves on the American cotton plantations they began to sing (verse 10). Although the word 'said' is used and not 'sing' in the NIV this part of the passage is written in a poetic style. It appears from the style of writing that the people were singing in the form of a lament. It had a rhythm of three beats followed by two that was a common style of the time. They were probably singing it as they worked, not the most encouraging words to work on!

It's hard to get an exact feel of the Hebrew but the following is a suggestion.

> *The strength of the labourers is giving out.*
> *There is so much rubble*
> *That on our own*
> *We cannot rebuild the walls.*

Our enemies said 'before they hear or see us
We will be there among them
We will kill them
And put an end to the work'.

Singing has been a way of expressing strong feelings and coping with life for a long time.

The Psalms are a classic example of just about every emotion from frustration to great joy. Modern spirituals which have evolved from those sung in slavery follow a similar tradition: such as 'Nobody know the trouble I've seen, nobody knows but Jesus'.

Nehemiah revealed his skills as a leader when he posted people on the walls in family groups (verse 13). Then he pointed out to them that God was on their side and it was their responsibility to fight for their families (verse 14).

Over the centuries there has been no institution which has survived the changes, pains and pressures of life so consistently as the family.

When God created Adam he said that it was not good for man to be alone and so the first family began (Gn.2:18).

When God spoke to Abraham he promised him he would be the father of many nations. Israel developed as a nation out of a family of twelve brothers.

A number of the Ten Commandments are concerned with the protection of the family, for example, honouring your father and mother and not committing adultery (Ex.20:12,14).

Love for family will keep folk pressing on when all else fails and Nehemiah recognized the fact. Jesus faced the cross because of his love for the Father and the family of man.

We become his relatives, brothers and sisters, when we accept him and his sacrifice for us (Jn.1:12). The church is the family of God's people and worth fighting for against all comers. Fight for the family!

Questions

1. What songs come to mind when you find life a struggle?

2. What weapons do you think God wants us to use in fighting for good?

3. How would you feel about giving your life for a member of your family?

History

Swords, spears, bows (verse 13) *The sword* is the most frequently mentioned weapon in the Bible and is often used as a symbol for the word of God (Ezk.21:9; Eph.6:17). It was seen as the main offensive weapon of war (Is.51:19; Je.14:15; 24:10; Ezk.7:15; 33:6).

The spear had a wooden shaft and a metal head – iron by this time – and was the main weapon of infantry or foot soldiers. It was sometimes seen as the symbol of royal authority (1 Sa.22:6; 26:7). The word used here can be translated 'pike' and it was used for hand-to-hand fighting whereas the javelin was thrown from a distance. It was about the height of an average man.

Bows were made of animal horn with strips of wood to make up the frame and were strung with sinew or gut. Archers were known as 'bow treaders' from the technique of pressing the bottom end with the foot in order to string it (Je.50:14). The bow was used for hunting as well as in times of war. As a weapon it came into general use in Israel when chariots came onto the scene because this required long-range weaponry. The archers from the tribe of Benjamin were quite famous for their skills (1 Ch.8:40; 12:2; 2 Ch.14:8.)

Biblical terms

Ten times over (verse 12) This is a Hebrew idiom used to say 'time and time again' (Gn.31:7,41; Nu.14:22; Jb.19:3; Dn.1:20).

Nehemiah 4:15–23

Swords and shovels

Doing God's will means faith and works – there has to be a balance between being warriors and workers.

No peace for the wicked or the godly either! It would be relatively easy to organize the people in Jerusalem into an army to guard the city, but then no work would be done. On the other hand they could get on with the work but be exposed to constant attack.
  Nehemiah had the answer, swords and shovels! Half the task force went on guard while the other half worked on the walls. Even the workers worked with one hand while they retained a sword in the other; from first thing in the morning until last thing at night.

 If there was an attack on another section of the wall the trumpet would sound and everyone would rally to the place of need knowing it might be them next time. In order to be constantly at the ready everyone kept their clothes on at night in order not to be caught 'napping', so to speak. The phrase 'the man who sounded the trumpet' (verses 18–20) is translated from the Hebrew word *shophar* meaning 'ram's horn' rather than the metal trumpet mentioned in the note on Ezra 3:10.

As well as being used in worship trumpets were used to sound a warning. The trumpeter had a key role to play in times of war (Jdg.3:27; 6:34; 7:18; 1 Sa.13:3; 2 Sa.20:1). The historian Josephus tells us that Nehemiah had trumpeters placed every 500 feet along the wall.[21]

Trumpeters gave the signal to break camp and to retreat from battle. The priest Phineas used one in Israel's battle with Midian (Nu.31:6) and priests again sounded the trumpets in the war between Abijah and Jeroboam (2 Ch.13:12–15).

When the battle began the *shophar* was sounded to signal the people to give the battle cry (Jos.6:5f; Jdg.7:16f). The trumpet was sounded again to announce the end of hostilities (2 Sa.18:16; 20:22). When you could no longer hear the *shophar* that was a sign of peace in Hebrew culture (Je.42:14).

When Paul talks about putting on the armour of God (Eph.6:10–20) the armour he mentions is all for guarding the front of the body and is a reminder of how much we need to protect each other when we are vulnerable. We all need each other. Once it is put on, Paul does not seem to suggest it should be taken off: like Nehemiah's builders, the Christian needs to be always at the ready.

The other issue which is highlighted here is the importance of getting on with the work God has called us to do. James said that 'faith without deeds is dead' (Jas.2:14–26). Christianity is not faith or action but faith in action, that is, swords and shovels.

Questions

1. What do you think is the equivalent of a sword and shovel for the Christian today?

2. How can you and I be ready at all times, on guard against the attacks of Satan?

3. What examples can you think of which illustrate faith in action in the church?

Personnel

Nehemiah's men (verse 23) Some versions use the word 'servants' but a more effective translation in modern idiom would be 'Nehemiah's lads' (see also 5:10, 16; 13:19). It makes clear the difference between Nehemiah's professional soldiers and the part-timers who would be regarded as a cross between the home guard (Dad's army) and the territorials.

A further distinction is made in verse 23 when Nehemiah refers to 'my brothers'. Were they his real brothers, his close companions or the officers compared with the men? If we compare 1:2, 5:10 and 7:2, it probably refers to his blood relatives including his brother, Hanani.

Biblical terms

Our God will fight for us (verse 20) This phrase is used only once in the whole of the NIV bible but the idea of God fighting for his people was a common Old Testament theme – 'the warrior god' (Ex.15:3; Is.42:13; Jer.20:11).

Even when he went for water (verse 23) The text is not clear at this point – translated literally it is 'each one his weapon water'. The translation in the NIV puts forward the possibility that this was the caution of experienced warriors, the kind of warrior that God instructed Gideon to select for battle (Jdg.7:5–7).

157

Nehemiah 5:1–5

The cry of the poor

Good news for the widow, the orphan and stranger is a condition
of restoration. In the same way that you show love for the least,
you show your love for God.

Poverty was caused by the fact that farmers were
not able to look after their fields because of the wall
building, so they did not have time to grow enough
food to live on. Also, trade would be bad because of
hostilities with the surrounding nations and in times
like that the poor are always the first to suffer.

There were three main reasons for poverty in Jerusalem at this
time. People deliberately had large families as an insurance for old
age; when there was no social security system you had to depend
even more on the family. Secondly, when times were hard and there
were no financial reserves it was a case of having to go into debt to
buy food or starve. Finally the Persian kings levied a tax known as
the king's tax, which everyone had to pay on their land whether
they could afford to or not.

What was annoying was the fact that the rich Israelites were
taking advantage of the poor in their need (verse 5). They were
from the same tribes, working together to restore Jerusalem. So it is

not really surprising that the poor began to complain, especially when they were forced into selling members of the family into slavery. 'A great outcry against their Jewish brothers' (verse 1) is the phrase used.

This phrase, 'a great outcry', has legal overtones (Gn.18:20–21; Ex.12:30; Jb.34:28). It arose out of an imbalance of resources between the common people and those referred to here as 'the Jews', although the NIV adds the word *brothers* (cf verse 5) to help clarify the relationship.

The phrase 'the Jews' seems to have some technical meaning (2:16; 5:17) which makes them distinct and separate from the ordinary people. The use may imply some form of middle-class culture within the Hebrew nation.

Jesus expressed much the same concern in stories like the Great Banquet, the Sheep and the Goats (Mt.25:31–46), and his reading of the Isaiah passage in Luke 4. There has to be good news for the poor if there is to be good news at all.

The same issue has been raised again and again throughout the history of the church. Self-interest amongst Christians has persistently maintained situations of injustice, not only in the world, but amongst God's people!

It brought about tension between slaves and their masters in the early church. It also raised serious questions regarding pay and conditions in the last century in Britain, for example between the owners of coal mines, cotton mills and factories and their workers, especially when many worshipped in the same churches. Some Lancashire mill owners would not hire people who did not, or would not, attend their chapels.

The Bible is consistent in its teaching on this issue, those people of God who 'have' are responsible for helping those who 'have not'. People of the Bible such as Amos and James express quite clearly God's concern when the religious rich exploit the godly poor (Amos 5:11–15; Jas.5:1–6).

God is a God of love, but he is also a God of justice and calls his people to reflect that in their own lives. Only then can we expect the kingdom on earth as it is in heaven.

As Mahatma Gandhi said 'There is enough for the world's need but not the world's greed'.

Questions

1. *Who are the widows, orphans and strangers in our society? How can we help them?*

2. *Why is the church in the West essentially middle-class in culture, for example council estate churches are usually very small if they exist at all?*

3. *How do you think we as Christians could do more to consider the needs of others instead of making sure we are comfortable?*

Biblical terms

The men and their wives (verse 1) The word 'men' would be better translated 'common people'. The most common use of the Hebrew word is 'people' or 'nation' (Ne.1:8; 9:22) and the translation into 'men' is misleading.

'And their wives' has an unusual emphasis because in Jewish culture of this period women would not normally be expected to speak, but things were so hard that even they cried out.

History

Mortgaging (verse 3) Borrowing by pledging was a common practice of the poor – pledging property and/or family members – in order to buy food or borrow money to pay taxes (2 Ki.4:1–2).

The law on this procedure was carefully balanced to ensure that there should be no long-term hardship as a result. Seven years was the maximum time in slavery for debt (Ex.21:2–11; Dt.15:12–18) then the person was to be released. A similar law applied to property (Lv.25:10–33; Ezk.18:7). It should be noted that 'daughters' are mentioned specifically in verse 4 because they were especially at risk. They could be made to marry the owner or one of his sons. This would make it next to impossible for the daughter to gain her freedom (cf Ex.21:7–11). The word 'mortgage' is only used in this sense in this verse of Nehemiah.

The basic problem was the age-old one; people will ignore the law if they can get away with it and there is financial advantage in doing so.

The king's tax (verse 4) This was a land tax according to the amount of land held. In the position of governor, Nehemiah would be responsible for collecting it and paying it to the king (after deducting his own expenses).

Taxes were an essential part of the economics of the Persian Empire and around 20 million Darics a year were collected. Any refusal to pay was seen as rebellion. The basic moral question is who got the money and how was it used? Little of the money collected ever found its way back to the provinces of the Empire. The majority found its way into the coffers of the king, his family and the political elite.

The rate of interest on loans at the time of Cyrus and then Cambyses ran at about 40–50%! Clay tablets from the *Elam* culture of this period, discovered in Persepolis, record that farmers were required to pay a tax of one-tenth of their sesame, one-tenth of their wine, and one-thirtieth of their grain.[22]

This form of taxation led to an accumulation of wealth for the already wealthy and increased debt and hardship for the poor. Documents from Babylon show that many were unable to redeem back their property and were forced to sell their children into slavery. Many poor people escaped to the big cities to avoid having to pay their debts.[23]

Nehemiah 5:6–13

Justice for all

If there is no justice for all then there is no justice at all – just ice.

Not only were the wealthy taking the poor into slavery, they were selling them to foreigners (verse 8). This form of oppression made it much harder for them to be bought back. It also gave the other nations the opportunity to have a laugh at Israel's expense.

Nehemiah, like God, heard the cry of the poor in Jerusalem and pointed out the injustice of the behaviour of the wealthy. You can sense his frustration when he points out that as fast as he and his friends were buying the poor out of slavery others in positions of power were forcing the poor back into servitude again (verse 8).

Nehemiah called for a cancellation of all debts and received a very positive response when everyone said, 'Amen', and did as they had promised (verse 13).

Jesus tells a parable which reflects Nehemiah's sentiments. He tells of a man who had a great debt cancelled and then, in turn, had a man imprisoned for being unable to repay him a much smaller amount (Mt.18:23–35). Jesus was speaking of forgiveness at the time and it is an important reminder to each one of us that God has cancelled our debts because Jesus paid the price on the cross. The call is to forgive others as God has forgiven us.

It is not helpful for the poor to be lectured on why they are in a mess. That is rather like Aesop's fable of the drowning man. While the man is drowning someone leans over the water's edge and says to him, 'You really should have learned to swim before you went in there!' Nehemiah calls on the people to 'walk in the fear of God' (verse 9) to avoid giving the enemy an opportunity to take advantage. If we do not attempt to practise God's justice all we have left is 'just ice'.

Questions

1. *Do you think Christians should help the poor if their poverty is a result of their own bad management of money? How?*

2. *What do you think is the difference between a human sense of justice and God's justice?*

3. *'Why should I share what I have with other people, after all, I have worked hard for it?' What would you say to someone in the church who said that to you?*

History

Usury (verse 7) The lending of money and charging of interest has always been legal. However, what was not allowed under Jewish law was attempting to make a profit out of a fellow Jew's poverty and distress. According to the law, the money should be lent without charging interest if it was for someone undergoing hard times (Ex.22:25; Lv.25:35–38; Dt.15:7–8; 23:19).

Biblical terms

We have bought back (verse 8) In Jewish law it was the responsibility of the nearest blood relative or kinsman to act as 'redeemer', that is, to buy back property or people of the family sold in hard times.

163

One of the most well-known accounts of this is in the book of Ruth, where Boaz assumes the responsibilities of kinsman and brings Ruth out of poverty back into a family (Ru.3:9,12; 4:1,3,6,8,14). Here Nehemiah takes on the role of the redeemer. Both Jeremiah and Isaiah portray God as the redeemer or kinsman of his people (Is.41:14; 43:14; 44:6,24; 47:4; 48:17; 49:7,26; 54:5,8; 59:20; 63:16; Je.50:34).

Jesus becomes the ultimate redeemer as he takes on the role of the nearest kinsman to the whole world. He has bought the world back from sin by his own blood (Lk.24:21; Gal.3:13–14; 1 Pet.1:18; Rev.5:9).

Shook Out the Folds (verse 13) The symbolism of what Nehemiah did was clear to those around him. In those times people would keep personal belongings and money in a pocket in the folds of their outer garments or robes.

So, by shaking the folds to show he had nothing left he made a significant statement about the results of ignoring his call to help the poor. They would have nothing left and neither God nor his people would be their blood relations.

Nehemiah 5:14–19

Practise what you preach

People are more convinced by what is said if they also see those who say it putting it into action in their own lives.

Nehemiah puts into action what he preaches by not claiming the *Governor's Food Allowance* (verses 14, 18). The governor of an area had the right to deduct from taxes collected for the king his own living allowance and expenses and those of his household. Because of the hardships on the people Nehemiah did not claim his entitlement (compare with Solomon: 1 Ki.4:22–23).

The previous governors (verse 15) have been identified through recent archaeological evidence. In 1974 a number of clay seals were found and examined by Nahmar Avigad.[24] One had the inscription *YHD* (the Persian name for the province of Judah) on it and is sixth or early fifth century BC. From the new evidence Avigad names the governors as El Nathan, Yeho'ezer, Ahazai and then Nehemiah.

Nehemiah could have exercised his right as governor to collect his salary from the taxes (1 Cor.9:8–15) but, like any good leader, he led by example and denied himself the right in order to avoid imposing further suffering on the poor. Wherever he got his money from it was not through taxation, even though he had to feed an extra 150 people 'at my table' (verse 17). It was considered a privilege to eat at the table of the king or some high official, like eating at the captain's table on board ship and it was a common practice for the ruler (for example 2 Sa.9:7,13; 19:28,33; 1 Ki.10:5; 1 Ki.18:19; Dn.1:5–15). Jesus tells a parable on the subject (Lk.14:7–14; compare with Lk.22:27–30).

This account of Nehemiah's conduct is taken from a personal diary and not from a public proclamation. He seems to have worked on the basis of not only 'do what I say, but follow my example'. He did not shout from the rooftops about his behaviour, neither buying up land, nor claiming entertainment expenses: his only concern was what God thought about his conduct (verse 19).

I have been in many places where items of furniture have plaques on them proclaiming the giver. Sometimes phrases like, 'To the glory of God', are used but normally in smaller lettering than the name of the person who made the donation.

Surely if we practise what we preach then we should be concerned to see God's name in large letters and not be concerned with gaining approval for ourselves?

People are much more convinced of the effect Jesus has had on our lives by our actions than our words.

When Peter and John put their faith into practice before the Jewish high council, the Sanhedrin, their behaviour led others to the conclusion that they had been with Jesus (Acts 4:13). It is not a case of words *or* actions but words *and* actions. Practise what you preach.

Questions

1. *Which is most important to you, to have the approval of others or God's approval? Why?*

2. *Have people asked you about your faith because of your actions?*

3. *What makes the church different from everybody else?*

Coins of the realm

Shekel (verse 15) A shekel of silver weighed about half a kilogramme. At this time a sheep cost three shekels and you could buy 20 pints of wine for a shekel. The verb *shaqal* in Hebrew means 'to weigh' or 'to pay', so it can be understood why the shekel became the basic monetary unit in Jewish culture, as well as the basic unit of weight. Abraham weighed out 400 shekels to purchase the *Cave of Machpelah* (Gn.23:16). Jeremiah weighed out 17 shekels to his cousin to buy the *Field of Anathoth* (Jer.32:9f). In this passage it is not really clear whether the shekels referred to are coins or weight of silver. What we do know is that they were not Median shekels because these were never used in Palestine (see also Ne.10:32).

Biblical terms

A hundred and fifty Jews and officials (verse 17) A stricter translation of this text is 'one hundred and fifty men' which implies that there may well have been women, and possibly children, present. This would make more sense of the amount of food supplied each day (verse 18) which some scholars have suggested was enough to feed 500 people.

Nehemiah 6:1–14

Intimidation

Pressure from people around us to see things their way, and through intimidation, the call to compromise and time-wasting have consistently been three of the most difficult traps to avoid in following God's way.

Three plots of varying subtlety were tried in order to trap Nehemiah. The first was to try to lure him away from Jerusalem (verse 2). The second was to accuse him of rebellion against the Persian Empire (verse 6). The third was to get him to sin by entering the area of the Temple where only a priest could go: for everyone else it could invoke the death penalty (verse 10; see Nu.1:51; 3:10; 18:7).

The open gates were the enemies' last chance of really being able to get at Nehemiah's people. Once the gates were completed (Ne.7:1) it would be much harder to carry out an effective attack. There is a touch of sarcasm in Nehemiah's response that if he meets with them the work will suffer (verse 3) when that is exactly what the opposition were trying to achieve.

Shemaiah is hired to trick Nehemiah, as a layman, into entering the Temple. It is not clear who Shemaiah is (verse 10), nor his actual job or position, other than to be a false prophet, although we are given details of his family.

Why Shemaiah was housebound is a puzzle. Had he committed some sin that restricted his movements? Was he carrying out a form of prophetic symbolism, for example, 'As I am housebound so should Nehemiah be shut in the Temple?' Or was he disabled in some way through illness? We can only guess.

His prophecy is given in verse in a poetic style that was popular at the time. However, it did not fool Nehemiah who sidestepped the trap and followed up with a prayer against intimidation (verse 14).

If the devil cannot get you to do anything else he will try to waste your time in unimportant activities.

Rumour and gossip conveying false information have also worked well in bringing the church into disrepute. Notice how quickly the media pick up scandal involving Christians and how slow they are to report good news.

It is also important to know where to draw the line as to how far we can go in our behaviour as Christians before we go too far.

Intimidation can make me drink more than I should, say more than I should and react in a way that I should not.

James gives very good practical advice, 'Resist the devil, and he will flee from you. Come near to God and he will come near to you' (Jas.4:7–8).

Questions

1. Have you experienced pressure from non-Christian friends to do something you know you should not do? If so, how did you handle it?

2. When is temptation hardest to resist in your life?

3. On what basis should the church decide where to draw the line between what is right and wrong?

Geography

The Plain of Ono (verse 2) The tower of Ono was near to Lod (where Israel's main airport, Ben Gurion, is situated today) about 25 miles north-west of Jerusalem (7:37; 11:35). The plain of Ono was also called the *Valley of Craftsmen*. It was a semi-neutral area between Judah and Samaria which is why it was suggested as a meeting place, although, because it was a day's journey from Jerusalem, it would mean Nehemiah would still be taking something of a risk travelling there.

History

An Unsealed Letter (verse 5) This was a piece of papyrus or pottery with no seal on it. The aim was for anyone who came in contact with it to be able to read it and know what was in it, and Sanballat intended Nehemiah to know that when he received it. In other words it was a thinly-veiled threat.

Personalities

Shemaiah (verse 10) the name does occur elsewhere referring to a Levitical role. It was a name representative of a prophetic responsibility. Then a descendant of King David of the same name is also mentioned (1 Ch.3:22; 1 Ch.9:14; 15:8; Ne.11:15; 1 Ki.12:22; Je.26:20; 29:4–7).

Noadiah (verse 14) Some have suggested that she may have been Shemaiah's wife but there is no real evidence for this. Very little is known about her except that she was a prophetess.

Women played an important role in prophecy in the Bible. Other prophetesses mentioned include Miriam (Ex.15:20), Deborah (Jdg.4:4), Huldah (2 Ki.22:14), Anna (Lk.2:36) and Jezebel (Rev.2:20).

Nehemiah 6:15–16

It is finished!

Even the most formidable of tasks, undertaken in the most difficult of circumstances, can be achieved with God's help.

Within six months of hearing of the sad state of Jerusalem Nehemiah had responded to the call and completed the task. At this time the wall was about 2,600 metres in circumference, unless the western hill was included, in which case it was around 4,100 metres.[25]

The wall was completed in just fifty-two days by perfume-makers, goldsmiths, priests and women, all working under the firm conviction that God was on their side. Josephus the historian claims the wall took two years and four months to finish.[26] It must be said, however, that he probably guessed this because the wall of Jerusalem was larger in his own time. Fifty-two days seems a reasonable time in which to complete the size of wall involved, bearing in mind that much of it was repaired rather than built from scratch. (Josephus made more than a few mistakes over dates, for example he put Nehemiah in the reign of Xerxes.)

The word 'completed' (verse 15) is the Hebrew word *shalam* that comes from the same root as the word *shalom* and literally means 'to be at peace', or 'to be whole'. Usually it is translated, 'to be restored', 'finished', 'completed'.

The word is used in the same sense when Solomon completed the building of the Temple (2 Ch.5:1) and to describe the foundations of the Temple (Ezr.5:16). It is only used on one other occasion when God speaks of finishing a king's reign (Dn.5:26).

The knock-on effect of the completion of the wall was that Nehemiah's enemies realized they had lost their battle with him because God was on his side (verse 16).

Jesus reflects the same sense of completing the task in his prayer to the Father (Jn.17:4) and when he finally triumphs over death on the cross his cry is, 'It is finished' (Jn.19:30).

It has been the hallmark of Christians over the centuries that when God was on their side anything was possible. The writer Rudyard Kipling once wrote that there is only one thing more frightening than a charge of Dervishes under the leadership of young cavalry officers, and that is a group of Presbyterians rising from their knees and prayer convinced they are about to do the will of the Lord!

After years of hard slog William Wilberforce heard on his death-bed that the slave trade had been abolished and his task was completed. Gladys Aylward was turned down for missionary work but she went anyway, convinced that God had called her even if others did not recognize it. Martin Luther King gave his life for a vision from God of a day when everyone would be treated equally. Others, inspired by his example, carry on the struggle.

We are all called to proclaim the good news of Jesus Christ, regardless of background and ability, and there can be no rest until we too can say 'it is finished'.

Questions

1. What is your response to the phrase, 'When the going gets tough the tough get going'?

2. When you face an impossible task how do you react?

3. Has your church achieved something against impossible odds? If so, how did non-Christians react?

Times and seasons

25th of Elul (verse 15) The sixth month of the year, in our calendar mid-September 445 BC.

Some have suggested the exact date was 2nd October.[27] In this view it is estimated that the work had begun on 11th August (if you include sabbaths) and completed 52 days later. But the month of *Elul* corresponds to August/September, and that would make the date too late.

Nehemiah 6:17–19

Blood is thicker than water

Close family ties can, and often do, pull people away from practising the godly life and loyalty to God.

As we have already noted in chapter 4, family loyalty and support are normally very strong. In the previous situation Nehemiah had used this to encourage the people to carry on at a time when morale was low. Now it was working against him. The fact that 'blood is thicker than water' was causing Nehemiah a problem. Letters and information were being passed on to the opposition, Tobiah in particular, largely because of family ties (verses 17–18).

Arah (verse 18) is mentioned in Ezra 2:5 and Nehemiah 7:10. It appears that Shemaiah, the son of Shecaniah, the son of Arah, was the guard on the East Gate (Ne.3:29). His sister married Tobiah and their son Jehohanan married the daughter of Meshullam. Meshullam was the son of Berekiah whom we find was the son of Meshezabel. He worked on the section of the wall next to the Fish Gate (Ne.3:4).

With these family ties it was clear why some Jewish nobility kept in close contact with Nehemiah's enemies (see also Ne.13:28). Close friends and family enticing people away from God must have been a persistent problem because there is a whole section on this in the book of Deuteronomy 13:6–11 where the tension is considered serious enough to warrant the death penalty.

It was the blood ties between Barnabas and his nephew, John Mark, which led to a disagreement with Paul and led to their splitting up (Acts 15:36–41). Jonathan overcame his family ties in order to ensure fair play for the future King David (1 Sa.20:1–4).

The same conflicts of interest still arise amongst Christians. Usually it is because a Christian is married to a non-believer. It can also be a problem when a person in the family who is not a Christian forces the believer to choose between what they want and God's will.

Jesus warned this would happen and calls on people to choose where their commitment lies, family or faith (Mt.10:34–39).

Questions

1. Have you been asked by a close family member to choose between them and God? What was your response?

2. Do you feel family should come first; if not why?

3. Can you think of instances in the church where family loyalties within the church have got in the way of the will of God?

History

Under oath (verse 18) Literally 'masters of the oath' and normally meaning 'sworn associates' or 'confederates'. It implies clan loyalties through blood ties, and/or a political affiliation (for other texts regarding oaths see the note on Ezra 10:5; also Ne.5:12; 10:29; 13:25).

Nehemiah 7:1–3

Shut that door!

A wall is only as strong as its weakest point. A chain is only as strong as its weakest link, and God's people are only effective when they guard each other's weak spots.

Nehemiah placed his brother in charge of the city because he was family, but justifies it by commending him as a godly man (verse 2). The NIV adds 'and Hananiah', to the verse, although it offers the alternative 'or Hanani, that is' as a footnote. It is unlikely that Nehemiah would have appointed two men, especially as their names are variations of the same name – the one is a longer form of the other.

'And' is translated as 'namely' in Ezra 8:18: 'the son of Israel, namely Sherebiah'(RSV). So I suggest in the same way in Nehemiah it should read 'my brother, namely Hanani or Hananiah...charge over Jerusalem'. It also makes sense of why Nehemiah had to comment on his brother's faithfulness and God-fearing nature, to avoid being accused of family favouritism.

Now that the gates were in place it was important to guard them. The city-wall gatekeepers mentioned here (verse 3) have a different task to the Temple gatekeepers (verse 45). A full description of their duties is given in 1 Chronicles 9:17–27 (see the note on Ezr.2:42).

It was no use having good solid walls if the gates were not guarded and it required godly people to ensure the city was safe. Jesus uses similar imagery when speaking of the good shepherd who guards the gate to the sheep (Jn.10:7–9).

We all need people we can rely on: the climber depends on the person holding the rope; passengers depend on the driver of a vehicle and Christians on the rest of their fellow-believers, especially those in positions of responsibility.

If there is an area of weakness it should be dealt with. Paul writes in his letter to the Galatians on the subject of temptation, being on watch and how to deal with open doors to sin. He says, 'if someone is caught in a sin, you who are spiritual should restore him gently. But watch yourself, or you also may be tempted' (Gal.6:1). Shut that door!

Questions

1. Who should respond to issues of weakness in the church and how?

2. What do you do to safeguard your own life against temptation?

3. How do you think God protects us against attack from our enemies?

Times and seasons

Until the sun is hot (verse 3) It may mean 'until the late morning' when the sun gets hot but there is another use of the phrase in the Old Testament: the time set aside for an after-lunch nap (Gn.18:1; 1 Sa.11:9,11; 2 Sa.4:5).

Nehemiah 7:4–72

Family trees

Can you prove you belong?

The walls were rebuilt, the gates were in place and now the houses needed to be repaired ready for people to re-occupy the city. Then Nehemiah found the family trees of those who had come back first from captivity in Babylon (verse 5).

Ten groups of people are mentioned starting with the leaders who came back with Zerubbabel in the first return. Twelve men are named (verse 7), possibly to represent the twelve tribes as separate entities, although the ten tribes of the northern kingdom, captured in 722 BC, seem to have disappeared or been assimilated by this period.

Next in the list come the families or clans. This includes the numbers of each family who had returned. They are identified by where they originally came from.

The next group is a 'who's who?' (including those who could not prove their ancestry; verses 61–65) providing a 'who does what' list of those who served in the Temple (verses 39–60).

Animals are also mentioned because they measure not only wealth but also will provide food for the people (verses 68–69).

This list is almost identical with the one in Ezra 2:1–70, with one or two variations. The significance of it is not the differences, but where the list occurs in each man's account. Nehemiah's first concern was to rebuild the wall and he records this first; whereas for Ezra a list of those who have already returned to Jerusalem has priority in his account. Now the wall has been completed and it is time to set about rebuilding the people of God.

Family trees are frequent right through the Bible; even Jesus' family tree is included (Mt.1; Lk.3). Most of us tend to skip them as dull and uninteresting, but what if it was your family tree, a list of all your ancestors?

Many folk today go to a lot of time and expense to discover who their ancestors were and where their roots are. They feel the need to prove where they belong. When we accept the sacrifice of Jesus personally and allow him to take control of our lives we become family with him. How do we prove we belong? Jesus said, 'by their fruit you will recognize them' (Mt.7:20) when warning those who would claim to belong to him. So what is the fruit which tells you someone is a Christian, a member of the family of Jesus. Paul gives a list in Galatians 5:22–23.

Questions

1. If I had to prove I was a child of God in order to get into heaven how would I?

2. Who are you related to in the kingdom of God and how can you prove it?

3. How does your church decide who can be a member?

History

The houses had not yet been rebuilt (verse 4)
Houses have already been mentioned in verse three so it is obvious that this does not mean there were no houses at all.

Some scholars say that the word 'house' would be better translated 'family' (see Dt.25:9; Ru.4:11;

Pr.24:27) and this is a possibility.

Alternatively, what it does suggest is that because of the priority of rebuilding the wall there had as yet been no major rebuilding of homes. In modern terms they were probably getting ready to declare the city of Jerusalem a 'major housing action area'. Re-population must wait until later (chapter 11).

Personalities

Nehemiah (verse 7) This is not Nehemiah, the cupbearer, but another by the same name who returned with Sheshbazzar and Zerubbabel in the first Return.

Senaah (verse 38) The name means *hated* and some think that the implication is that it is not actually a place but refers to a lower class. Whoever, or whatever they were they certainly did their fair share of work on the wall (3:3; Hassenaah can be translated as 'the senaah').

Biblical terms

To assemble (verse 5) The Hebrew word used can mean 'to gather into someone's arms' or 'bosom' (Is.40:11; 54:7; see also Ezr.7:28; 8:15; 10:7,9; Ne.1:9; 5:16; 13:11).

The use of the word has much in common with the word 'church', that is, the people of God assembled for God's purposes.

The list of the men of Israel (verse 7) The list is very similar to the one in Ezra and some scholars have debated whether the list in Ezra 2 came first, or did Nehemiah have the original? Why is there a difference between Ezra 2:68f and Nehemiah 7:69f for instance? Of the forty-nine numbers in Ezra 2:3-67 only twenty-six are the same as those here in Nehemiah. Some have argued that as Nehemiah's figures are sometimes larger that it may be a revision of original estimates at a later date. One reason for slight differences of emphasis in the two lists could be to do with why and how the lists are used.

In the book of Ezra only those who can prove they are Jewish are allowed to participate. In Nehemiah the emphasis is on the selection of people to live in the city of Jerusalem.

Nehemiah 8:1–3

Hear the word

Listen and take time to understand God's word.

The people had returned to the land of Israel, restored the Temple to its former glory, the city walls had been rebuilt, and now it was time to rebuild the people of God.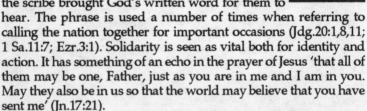

The people gathered 'as one man' (verse 1) as Ezra the scribe brought God's written word for them to hear. The phrase is used a number of times when referring to calling the nation together for important occasions (Jdg.20:1,8,11; 1 Sa.11:7; Ezr.3:1). Solidarity is seen as vital both for identity and action. It has something of an echo in the prayer of Jesus 'that all of them may be one, Father, just as you are in me and I am in you. May they also be in us so that the world may believe that you have sent me' (Jn.17:21).

The phrase 'able to understand' (verse 2) is the Hebrew word *shema* (to hear). Used here it means literally 'all that could *hear* with understanding'. It is an interesting word because there is no Hebrew word for 'obey'. The implication is if you hear then you should obey, like the mother who implies the same when she shouts at a disobedient child: 'didn't you hear me?' (Ne.9:29).

Every Jewish child, even today, is expected to learn *The Shema*

(Hear O Israel; Dt.5:1). It is a prayer that is learned and repeated regularly in just the same way as Christians learn the Lord's Prayer.

A significant part of rebuilding the nation was to hear God's word with the implied emphasis on obeying it. What is worth noting is that they listened attentively (verse 3) from daybreak until noon. These days people sometimes complain when preachers preach beyond fifteen minutes!

Times have changed and so have cultures and customs, but there is a clear statement in Isaiah that 'the word of God stands for ever' (Is.40:8).

Jesus compares everyone who heard his words with either a wise or a foolish builder. The wise one built on a solid foundation and survived the storms, the foolish builder ignored him and built on sand, and what he built fell down (Mt.7:24).

If Christians today want to build their lives on solid rock then, amid all the changes, one challenge is still the same. Hear the word of the Lord, and to hear is to obey.

Questions

1. *Do you believe all the Bible as we have it is God's word?*

2. *How much time do you take to listen to what God is saying into your life?*

3. *If God's word should be obeyed why do so many in the church ignore it?*

Geography

The square before the Water Gate (verse 1) As has already been noted (see note on Ne.3:26) this was a regularly used place for public gatherings.

What is of additional significance is the fact that water is often seen as a symbol of God's blessing. It can also be used to describe spiritual refreshing (for example, Ps.23:2; Is.32:2; 35:6-7; 41:18).

Also associated with water is cleansing (Ex.29:4; Nu.8:7) and the special washing on the Day of Atonement (Lv.16:4,24,26). This was the seventh month (verse 2) and the Day of Atonement was held on the tenth day.

Jesus would later use the expression 'living water' when referring to the Holy Spirit (Jn.7:38).

Times and seasons
Seventh Month (verse 2) See the note on Ezra 3:1.

Nehemiah 8:4-8

Making sense

When you understand God's word, it requires a response.

The reading of the Law was done from a wooden platform (verse 4). Literally *a wooden tower*, it must have been fairly large to hold thirteen men. With the wall and the gate behind it acting as a sounding board, the acoustics would probably be quite good. What we have here may be the forerunner of the pulpit, but the word 'tower' gives us more of a clue to its symbolism.

Towers were used to keep watch from, and to give warning to others. There was often a tower in a vineyard to protect it from unwelcome guests (Is.27:3; Israel was seen as God's vineyard). Ezekiel spoke of the role of the watchman in the tower (Ezk.3:17; 33:2; 33:6-7).

Reading the Law to the people was like reminding someone of their wedding vows. This is more than just words, it is the reminder of the depth of relationship and commitment between two people. The image of God and his people as bridegroom and bride is a recurring concept in the Bible.

So as we hear and understand God's word it reminds us that we too are in a covenant relationship with him: to love, honour and obey.

Questions

1. Why do people read the Bible?

2. How does it affect you when something suddenly becomes clear to you?

3. Using the analogy of marriage, why do Christians break their promises to God when he keeps his to them?

Biblical terms

Positions in worship (verses 5–7) As Ezra opened the book (in reality he would have unrolled a scroll) the people *stood* (verse 5) and they remained standing (verse 7) for about five to six hours. Standing was something that was done in the presence of a king (Dn.1:19: compare with Dt.29:10; 2 Ch.18:18).
The NIV translates Dn.1:19 as 'the King's service' but it means literally 'standing before the king' (see the King James version for example).

They responded with their *arms lifted up* (verse 6). This was a classic Hebrew position for prayer (Ex.9:29, 33; 17:11; 1 Ki.8:54; 2 Ch.6:12–13; Ezr.9:5; Ps.28:2; 44:20; 63:4; 88:9; 134:2; 141:2; 143:6; Is.1:15). Psalm 119:48 is a specific response to the Law of God, and Lamentations 1:17 may give some clue to the origin of the position in begging or pleading.

Then in verse 6 they *bowed down* and prostrated themselves, *faces to the ground* (see note on Ezra 9:5).

The leaders 'instructed the people in the law while the people were *standing there*' (verse 7– my italics).

Nehemiah 8:9–12

Don't be sad

The joy of the Lord is your strength.

The people are gathered together to celebrate the Feast of Booths or Tabernacles (see the note on Ezr.2:4) and then they began to mourn and weep (verse 9). Tabernacles was normally regarded as a time of rejoicing so it seems strange that the people reacted in this way, especially as they had just observed the Day of Atonement when they would have made amends for wrongdoing.

Responding to God's word in this way is not unlike King Josiah's reaction on hearing God's word read out (2 Ch.34:19). The high priest had just rediscovered the Book of the Law while spring-cleaning the Temple. Do you ever lose your Bible?

It is interesting how often in Ezra and Nehemiah strong emotions are expressed: anger, sadness, hate and then joy.

The joy of the Lord is spoken of at a time of intense pressure. It was not some happy, clappy, praise meeting. The people had just stood for the best part of five or six hours! Warren W. Wiersbe, in his book on Nehemiah[28], speaks of the move from conviction to cleansing and then on to celebration. This was the line taken by Nehemiah when he called on the gathering to move on to celebration: 'The joy of the LORD is your strength' (verse 10).

The word for 'joy' used here only occurs in three other places (1 Ch.16:27; Ezr.6:16; Ne.12:43,44). The Hebrew word means 'to be jubilant' (especially if you have just succeeded), 'to rejoice', 'be joyful' and seems to mean 'a spiritual joy' in particular (see the note on Ezr.3:12,13).

So the implication here would appear to be that with God there is joy-giving strength. Without God there is misery leading to weakness and apathy.

The Greek word for 'joy' used by Paul in describing the fruits of the Spirit (Gal.5:22) is also a joy based on experiences of God.

The apostle Paul wrote from prison, on trial for his life, in a similar vein – 'rejoice in the LORD always. I will say it again: rejoice!' (Phil.4:4). In Liverpool, another tough place to be sometimes, there is a saying, 'you have to laugh otherwise you cry'.

I think that these are all attempts at expressing the same realization. When we take a positive response to depression, oppression and outright times of trial, we can discover not only relief from the temptation, but an incredible ability to draw strength from a joy from God: a joy which does not depend on everything going smoothly all the time. It is not a joy *afterwards* but *during* times of trial.

The call is still the same: no matter how tough life is don't be sad, remember the joy of the Lord is your strength.

Questions

1. *Does your Christian life go up and down according to the way you feel? How do you deal with it?*

2. *What do you think is the difference between joy and happiness?*

3. *The church often grows significantly in times of persecution and hardship. Why?*

History

Governor (verse 9) Some translations use the word
Tirshatha, meaning 'governor' and not just a name
(see the note on Ezr.2:63). It comes from the New
Persian *tarash*, and literally means 'to cut'. The word
is used in Ezra 2:63, Nehemiah 7:65, 70; 8:9; 10:1 to
mean 'someone who is to be feared or respected'. It
is not used anywhere else, and some manuscripts omit the name
Nehemiah.

Some have implied that Nehemiah's name was added later
because this is the only occasion when Ezra and Nehemiah are
recorded as being in the same place at the same time.

This is the first time in Nehemiah's diary of events that Ezra has
been mentioned and now they both appear together. Ezra had
arrived in Jerusalem some time before Nehemiah, so it does seem a
little strange that they had not worked together before this. Despite
this there is no real evidence to justify omitting one name or the
other from the text.

Nehemiah's main task was in the political arena, whereas Ezra
was specifically a religious leader. So it was only to be expected
that Ezra would be 'up-front' on this particular occasion (see the
note on Ne.12:26).

Biblical terms

Joy (verse 12) The Hebrew word is different from
the one used in verse 10 (also verse 17). The word
is usually translated as 'mirth', 'gladness', 'joy',
'happiness', 'gaiety', 'pleasure'. It has a significant
difference of emphasis. The joy here is based on
having a good time, 'enjoying yourself' rather than
'enjoying the Lord'.

So it is significant how much more frequently the word occurs in
the Old Testament – over thirty times (for example Ne.8:17; 12:43;
Jon.4:6).

Nehemiah 8:13–18

Outdoor pursuits

God does offer security, but in himself, not in the things of this world.

Living in temporary shelters was a reminder to the Jews that when the Lord delivered them from slavery in Egypt they had to rely totally on him. Coming out of Egypt was only the beginning. Too much reliance on possessions for their security led to selfishness and spiritual apathy. The second Captivity was a harsh reminder of what happens when God is ignored. So the Feast of Tabernacles was a symbolic way of setting aside the material comforts of life in order to come into the presence of God.

It is called the feast of the seventh month (verse 14). This is also called the Festival of Booths and has already been mentioned in the note on Ezra 2:4. The date is the day after the Law was read (8:2) the second day of *Tishri*. The feast of Tabernacles (Succoth in Hebrew) should begin on the fifteenth day of the month (Lv.23:33; Nu.29:12).

For some reason which is not immediately obvious, the Day of Atonement (Yom Kippur) is not mentioned. Some scholars think that Ezra changed the dates: either that he celebrated Tabernacles from the third to the tenth day, or he moved the Day of Atonement from the tenth to the twenty-fourth day (9:1).

It is an interesting thought but if it were true then there was not enough time to celebrate an eight-day feast. What is more likely is Yom Kippur was not yet a fixed date in the Jewish calendar. Even in Zechariah's time the Day of Atonement is only mentioned by the month and not the date (Zc.7:5, 8:19).

Jesus talked of having no security in a house when someone asked to follow him (Mt.8:20). Others made excuses because their security was in possessions rather than Jesus.

Paul discovered the secret of a satisfied life by looking to God for his security. In prison, and on trial for his life, he wrote a letter to the church at Philippi. In it he spoke of joy (4:4), satisfaction (4:12), and the conviction that God would look after his people (4:19).

Israel had to come out of Egypt, Paul called on Christians not to compromise their faith with the call, "'Therefore come out from them and be separate,' says the LORD. 'Touch no unclean thing and I will receive you'" (2 Cor.6:17).

There are lots of ways in which we can come out. We can come out from the security of church buildings. We can come out from self-centred life styles. Then we can come into the presence of God.

Questions

1. *If you could have three things on a desert island what would you take with you?*

2. *Is it right for Christians to have plenty of everything? Why?*

3. *How important are church buildings to the Christian faith?*

Biblical terms

The Book of the Law of God (verse 18) There are generally four views of what this was: a collection of legal documents; the Deuteronomic laws; the Pentateuch (the first five books of the Bible); or the Priestly code of laws.

Paul uses the term frequently (Rom.7:22, 25; 8:7; for example). It appears to be inter-changeable with the phrase the 'Law of Moses' in the New Testament in referring to the Pentateuch (Lk.2:22; 24:44; Jn.7:23; Acts 13:39; 15:5; 28:23; 1 Cor.9:9; see the note on Ezr.6:18). So there is no reason whatsoever to suppose that Ezra could not have brought back the Pentateuch from Babylon.

The whole company that had returned from exile (verse 17) This phrase reveals an assumption which has been made before (Ezr.4:1, 4). That is, that there were no practising Jews who had remained behind in Judah, only those who had returned.

Geography

The Gate of Ephraim (verse 16) This gate appears to be close to the Fish Gate on the north wall and is mentioned in Nehemiah 3:3 (see the note on this verse). This is supported by Nehemiah 12:38 and 2 Kings 14:13 which suggests that it was about 600 feet from the Corner Gate.

Times and seasons

On the eighth day, in accordance with the regulation (verse 18) This was a solemn closing assembly following the reading of the Law. Eighth-day assemblies are mentioned in Numbers 29:35 and Leviticus 23:36. This is probably where Nehemiah is quoting from, although he does not say so specifically.

Nehemiah 9:1–5

The great confession

There can be no forgiveness until we are willing to say sorry.

The people gathered later in the month for a time of public confession, when they fasted and wore sackcloth (verse 1). Curiously, sackcloth or clothes are not mentioned anywhere else in Ezra or Nehemiah. It is rather a puzzle because the practice was well-known in the Old Testament.

Sackcloth was made of hair and used for sieving or straining liquids. The hair used was normally goats' hair which was black. It was also made into sacks for keeping grain in. The harshness of the cloth next to the body made it an effective aid to both mourning, suffering and repentance (for example, Est.4:1; Job 16:15; Is.3:24; 58:5).

Suffering as a form of penitence has been a common religious practice over the centuries. During the Middle Ages pilgrims going to Canterbury would wear sackcloth, some even crawled there on their hands and knees to heighten the experience – and the pain!

Also they separated themselves from all foreigners (verse 2). There is no reference here to Ezra's call to separate (Ezr.10). Some have speculated as to why Nehemiah does not connect the two occasions. It is my belief that there is no need to do so.

The first situation, in Ezra, involved men and women specifically within a family structure. Nehemiah's concern in this passage is the intermixing with foreigners in a time of confession for the nation of Israel, within an act of worship.

Although Deuteronomy 16:14 encourages aliens, or foreigners, to enjoy the celebration, can they take part in a time of confession for the nation?

Nehemiah appears to think not. This event is more likely to lead into the reforms which are recorded in chapter 13 than a direct reference to Ezra.

Confession is still considered an important part of public as well as private worship. After all, how can there be forgiveness if there is no confession of guilt?

James calls for believers to confess their faults to one another (Jas.5:16) and in 1 John we are told that when we confess our faults God is faithful to forgive (1 Jn.1:9).

Just because we are Christians does not mean we never have any problems, or that we never make any mistakes.

When God gave us a new start through his son Jesus he made us clean. But it is like having a bath, it does not mean that we will never have to wash again. There will be times when we have to wash the dirt off, say we are sorry and get right with God and the folk around us. The old saying is right; confession is good for the soul.

Questions

1. Why do you think some people feel it is necessary to suffer in some way before they can be forgiven by God?

2. What do you think it is that causes us to be so condemning of other people, while refusing to admit it when we make mistakes?

3. Should the church say sorry on behalf of a nation? (see 2 Ch.7:14)

Times and seasons

A quarter of a day (verse 3) The time taken to read from the Law is paralleled by the same experience in chapter 8, it was from early morning to midday. The main difference is that this time it is split into two halves. Half the time was spent in reading the Law and the other half in confession.

Personnel

The Levites (verse 4) The events of the previous chapter involved thirteen Levitical assistants. In this passage eight stood on the stairs and cried out to God (verse 4) and eight (some of whom were the same priests) gave out a call for people to stand up and praise God (verse 5). Five of those named were involved on the first occasion (8:4). As a result some feel that the two records actually describe the same event. However, to accept that is to ignore the fact that the focus was distinctly different in the two events.

The first was exclusively *to hear* God's word read out. The second began with prayer and fasting which led on to a time of general confession. Only after this was the Law *read*, not spoken (compare verse 3 with 8:3), followed by time spent in praise worship.

Nehemiah 9:6–31

Yesterday

It is good to remember the past, not with sentimentality, but to learn from it.

As part of their act of worship together the Levites lead the people in thanksgiving to God for all his goodness to them as a nation. They recall again their history as a nation and how God has been with them throughout. Their prayer of praise and thanksgiving divides into three themes:

The birth of the nation under God and the reasons for the first captivity in Egypt (verses 7–18).

The wanderings in the wilderness for forty years following the exodus from Egypt, and God's goodness, guidance and provision during that period (verses 19–23).

Israel's entry into the land that God had promised them, reflecting on Israel's unfaithfulness in times of plenty (verse 23–31).

There are times when we do not feel as close to God as we once were. Often it is when things are not as they should be.

When Israel was in Babylon people began to think about home in a very sentimental way (for example Ps.137), like a Welshman a long way from home on Saint David's day! What they had not learned from the past was that they were only in Babylon because they had ignored God. Time after time he had sent his prophets to speak to them and they had rejected them. So much so that Jesus told a parable about the tenants of the vineyard to make the point to Jewish listeners (Lk.20:9–16).

If we look back just to remember 'the good old days' it can prevent us from moving on to the place where God wants us to be. Lot's wife is a classic example of someone who looked back for the wrong reason and ended up going nowhere (Gn.19:17–26). The only good reason for looking back is to remember the goodness of God in times of testing, and to learn from the mistakes we have made.

Going the wrong way and learning from your mistake is discovery but repeating the experience is pure stupidity.

Questions

1. *How do you take time to remember the things God has done for you in the past?*

2. *When people look back do they remember the good or the bad experiences and why?*

3. *Do you think that the church has learned from the mistakes of the past? If not, why not?*

Geography

Ur of the Chaldeans (verse 7) See the note on Ezra 5:12.

Perizzites, Jebusites (verse 8) See the note on Ezra 9:1.

Girgashites (verse 8) The Bible records them as being descendants of Canaan (Gn.10:16). We know little else about them, other than one or two references in ancient Near Eastern manuscripts.[29]

Times and seasons

Sabbath (verse 14) This is the first mention of the Sabbath in either Ezra or Nehemiah. It seems unusual that, as a religious leader involved in reform, Ezra did not raise the issue of the Sabbath at all.

Nehemiah raises issues of the Sabbath in a number of verses between here and chapter 13 (10:31; 13:15–22).

The Hebrew word *shabbat* means 'to rest', 'cease' or 'desist' and is closely linked to the word *shibah* meaning 'the seventh'. So the Sabbath derives its name from the creation when God rested on the seventh day – Saturday. So what is good for God is good for his people and keeping the Sabbath becomes a law (Ex.20:8–11).

While the Jews operated a six-day working week the Babylonians used a five-day week system, although they did not adhere to it as strictly as the Jews. Once this holy day concept became law many Jewish scholars began to debate what could and could not be done on this day. For instance, it is forbidden to drag a chair because it is seen to create a furrow on an earth floor. So the person who does it is guilty of ploughing.

Carrying loads or trading on the day of rest was Nehemiah's primary focus. Jesus observed the Sabbath (Lk.4:16) but he did differ in his understanding of its purpose from some of the religious leaders of his day (Mt.12:1–14; Mk.2:23–28; Lk.6:1–11).

Christians later changed the day of rest from Saturday to Sunday and called it 'the LORD's day' (Rev.1:10). They did this in remembrance of the fact that Jesus rose from the dead on a Sunday.

This change in day did lead to some contention in the early days of the church (Rom.14:5).

Biblical terms

Bread from heaven (verse 15) The phrase is used in the Old Testament as an expression of God's provision for his people (for example, Ex.16:4; Pss.78:24; 105:40). It is also developed by Jesus in the New Testament (Jn.6:31–41; Rev.2:17).

The word translated 'bread' can also be translated 'food', which is a better way of describing *manna*. 'Manna' was not bread and the Hebrew word means 'what is it?' which was the Israeli reaction when they first encountered it in the wilderness.

Stiff necks (verses 16,17,29) The image used here is to express 'stubbornness' and 'rebellion' (Dt.9:6, 13; 10:16). The phrase 'stiff necked' developed from the experience of an ox resisting the person guiding it via the yoke on its neck. So people resisting God's will are refusing to be guided by him.

The phrase was popular in the Old Testament and is used several times. It is even translated into Greek in the New Testament (Acts 7:51).

Personalities

Abram (verse 7) Abraham was first called Abram. For the way his name was changed read Genesis 17:5.

Sihon (verse 22) Sihon was one of the Amorite kings and Heshbon was his capital city (Nu.21:31). It was a nation which conquered the Moabites (Je.48:45) and the Midianites (Jos.13:21). The kingdom covered an area to the east of the river Jordan halfway between Galilee and the Dead Sea. It went as far as the desert to the east, as far as the river Ammon in the south and the river Jabbok in the north. The country was given to the tribes of Reuben and Gad (Nu.32:33–38).

Later tradition claims that Sihon was the brother of King Og (*Babylonian Talmud, Niddah* 61a).

Og of Bashan (verse 22) King Og was an Amorite and king of Bashan (Nu.21:21–35). He belonged to what is believed to have been a tribe of giants. The nation was made up of over sixty cities. Og's lands were given to the half-tribe of Manasseh (Dt.3:13). His kingdom ran from the river Jabbok in the south to Mount Hermon in the north.

Og was famous for his bed made of iron (Dt.3:11). He is also mentioned in Pss.135:11 and 136:19–20.

Nehemiah 9:32–38

Today

God is not just a God of history, he is still present, powerful and dependable.

This section begins with the reminder, in the image of a marriage, that God is faithful to his covenant. The problem is not God but his people, they are the ones who are lacking in loyalty.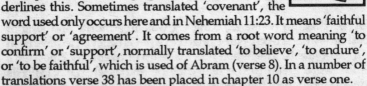

The phrase, 'a binding agreement' (verse 38) underlines this. Sometimes translated 'covenant', the word used only occurs here and in Nehemiah 11:23. It means 'faithful support' or 'agreement'. It comes from a root word meaning 'to confirm' or 'support', normally translated 'to believe', 'to endure', or 'to be faithful', which is used of Abram (verse 8). In a number of translations verse 38 has been placed in chapter 10 as verse one.

What is amazing is that God is still forgiving and faithful to his promises despite the failure, the foolishness and weakness of his people. The point is made very clearly in the imagery used in the story of Hosea and his wife, Gomer, in the book of Hosea. There God's relationship with Israel is compared with that of Hosea and Gomer. The overall theme is that the love of God is as real, meaningful and forgiving today as it was yesterday.

Questions

1. *How many times do you think you could forgive someone who has broken promises they had made to you?*

2. *Why is it that God keeps on loving us despite the way we
sometimes treat him?*

3. *Is there anyone in your experience who you feel you can
never forgive? Why?*

Biblical terms

Covenant of love (verse 32) The phrase translated
'abounding in love' in verse 17 uses the same word
chesed (see the note on Ezra 7:28).

Serve (verse 35) The Hebrew word means 'to serve
in a religious sense'. It can be translated 'to be subject to a conqueror' or 'to worship' (Ezr.4:11; 5:11; 6:18). This has
implications in the use of the word slave in the following verse.

Personnel

Slaves (verse 36) The same concept expressed here
is also found in Ezra 9:9. In Jewish law a Jew could
only be used as a slave for six years then they had to
be set free (Ex.21:2–11). The only exception to this
was when someone chose to remain in a state of slavery. Then the slaves had their ears pierced as a sign
of attaching themselves to the owner (Ex.21:6; Dt.15:17). Females
became the concubines of their master or one of his sons. They
experienced the same fate as female prisoners-of-war (Dt.21:10–14;
see also the note on Nehemiah 5:3).

The word meaning 'a bondservant' or slave' is used a number of
times (Ezr.9:8,9; Ne.5:18; 9:17). More literally it means 'someone
who is not his/her own master, but in the power of another'. So the
same word can mean those who are subject to a king or ruler.

Jews who became slaves in Israel usually did so mainly through poverty in the family. A slave was worth around thirty shekels (Ex.21:32) at a time when the average wage was around ten shekels a year. So this verse has in it the implication that the people are suffering a spiritual poverty because of disobedience. 'We are slaves today' (verse 36) 'because of our sins' (verse 37).

Fig. 9: King Darius with prisoners – 516 BC
(Taken from a rock face by a roadside in Iran)

Nehemiah 10:1–29

Forever

The promise to be faithful to God is a promise which should last, like his love, forever.

The reason the various leaders, officials, Levites and priests were gathered together, and named, was in order to carry out an oath of allegiance to God. It was very much a public act, naming names in order to ensure people kept their promises. Many of those mentioned are family names (fifteen of the twenty-one priestly names are family names and the leaders are mentioned almost completely by their family names). So what was promised was not just by individuals for themselves, but on behalf of complete families.

It is much more difficult to go back on your word in front of witnesses. You can be sure that if you do forget there will always be someone there to remind you.

The contract is with all those who have 'separated themselves' (verse 28). The words used here are words associated with divorce on the one hand, and holiness on the other. The call to separate themselves from other nations is a call, echoing Ezra (see the note on Ezr.10:11), to racial purity. But it was more than that, it was also a call away from idolatry. Idolatry often went hand in hand with mixing, especially through marriage, with other nations (for example 2 Ki.11:1–6). The word 'separate' implies the breaking off of a friendship. The promise was to put God and his Temple first and to have no other gods. Just like the marriage promise 'to forsake all others'.

That is what holiness is, to be set apart for God's purposes or 'elected'. The Jews sometimes mistook that calling to be set apart as a separation to be superior when in fact it was a call to service (see the note on Ezra 8:28).

Some scholars have suggested that this group included those from other nations who had converted to Judaism but the context makes it unlikely.[30]

The act of marriage is used frequently as an image of the covenant that God's people have with him. Jesus also uses the image of the church as his bride. The marriage ceremony is always a public act, promises are made in front of witnesses, names are named. It is intended to encourage people to keep their promises as well as allowing a man and a woman to make a covenant with each other.

The Christian is called upon to do the same: Paul says, 'That if you confess with your mouth, "Jesus is Lord," and believe in your heart that God raised him from the dead, you will be saved' (Rom.10:9). It is like marriage except that it is not, 'until death us do part', but forever!

Questions

1. Does God ever break his promises to us? If 'no', why not?

2. Does the church ever break its promises to him?

3. Can you think of times when you have made your stand publicly for Jesus? Why did you do it?

Biblical terms

Those who sealed it (verse 1) The use of the word seal only occurs here and in Nehemiah 9:38, although the practice of using a seal to authenticate a document was very common during this period of Israel's history. Thousands of seals have been recovered by archaeologists from the ancient Near East. Over 200 seals of Hebrew origin have been recovered, all with their owners' names on them.

Wax or clay was placed on a document and the owner's mark was imprinted on it as a sign of ownership to prove it was genuine (Je.32:11–14). It was also used to make it impossible to read a document without breaking the seal first. Jesus' tomb was sealed so that the Roman authorities would know if anyone had been tampering with it (Mt.27:66). The same thing happened with Daniel in the lions' den (Dn.6:17).

The seal was usually worn on a cord around the owner's neck, on a pin which would be worn on clothing or as a ring on the finger (Gn.38:18; Je.22:24).

A curse and an oath (verse 29) Taking an oath meant to use a curse (see the note on Ezra 10:5).

Nehemiah 10:30-40

A contract with God

Putting God first in all things is not just an ideal, it is an imperative.

'The house of our God' is a phrase which is used nine times in this passage. Neglect of the Temple was neglect of the covenant contract God had established with his people through Moses: a contract which is highlighted in the Decalogue (the Ten Commandments, Ex.20:2–17).

The nation had been called to *submit* themselves to a covenant with God. Then they were called upon to *separate* themselves from the surrounding nations in order to be used by God. Now the call is to *support* the work of God as they had promised to do. All of this required them keeping their contract with God.

The note on Nehemiah 9:14 comments on the Jewish concept of Sabbath. The seventh year, mentioned in verse 31 is a development of the same principle. It is a sabbatical year when even the land is given a rest: the 'fallow year' law (Ex.23:10–11; Lv.25:1–7).

The seventh year was also the year when debts were cancelled (Dt.15:1–18) and it was the time when Hebrew slaves were set free (Ex.21:2–11; Je.34:14). This 'seventh-year' principle was intended to ensure justice for all in terms of social as well as religious values.

Sadly it was not really observed (Je.34:8–16) because it affected people's pockets. Whenever cost is involved there seems to be compromise (Ne.5:6–13).

Giving was obviously a key concern of Nehemiah and so the tithe, or giving of a tenth is raised (verses 37–38). He reminds the people of their responsibility to give God the first fruits, not the last (verses 35–37), a law which had not been observed for some time.

Following on from the theme of giving, the people are called to tithe (Ne.12:44; 13:5). The failure to give to God is perceived to be the cause of crop failure as well as spiritual decline (Mal.3:10).

The people still had to pay other taxes to the Persian ruler (Ne.5:4) and before that to their own kings (1 Sa.8:15,17).

There is some debate about tithing in the New Testament as it appears that there is no specific command to Christians to tithe. The main references to tithing (Mt.23:23; Lk.11:42; 18:12) involve condemnation of the religious and self-righteous. The other passage in Hebrews 7:2–9 is about paying the priest Melchizedek.

The only other clear indicator of giving in the church comes from Paul (2 Cor.8 and 9). He appears to set no limit on giving and appeals to generosity of heart: 'God loves a cheerful giver' (2 Cor.9:7).

We live in a society today where it seems everyone is concerned with their rights. The difficulty is that there is not the same enthusiasm about our responsibilities. That was Haggai's criticism – God's people were making sure they were comfortable but they neglected his house, the Temple (Hg.1:3).

It is true that today there are too many neglected church buildings which could do with some time spending on them. However, that is not what Paul is speaking about when he echoes the cry of Haggai about the Temple.

The Temple of God (his house) under the new covenant in Christ is Christian believers. He was calling the Christians at Corinth to face up to their responsibilities when he wrote, 'Don't you know that you yourselves are God's temple and that God's Spirit lives in you ? If anyone destroys God's temple, God will destroy him; for God's temple is sacred, and you are that temple' (1 Cor.3:16).

The way to make sure we don't neglect God's house (us) is to keep our contact with him. Jesus said, 'If you love me, you will obey what I command' (Jn.14:15). It is just like the marriage contract – love, honour, and obey.

Someone once said that if you want real joy then you must put Jesus first, others second, and yourself last. That is our contract with God.

Questions

1. Why is it easier to remember how much someone owes me, rather than how much I owe them?

2. Why is finance often a problem for the church?

3. Are there opportunities for Christians to take up their responsibilities to God in practical ways in your community, and if so how?

Coins of the realm

A third of a shekel (verse 32) This was a tax which was imposed on all males over the age of twenty and paid once a year. It was initiated to pay for maintaining the Tabernacle (Ex.30:11–16; 38:25) and resurrected by King Joash in order to repair the Temple (2 Ki.12:4–15; 2 Ch.24:4–14).

It was probably encouraged by Nehemiah as part of his purge on mixing and compromising the faith of Israel (Ne.13:30). He would probably have objected to jumble sales for church funds!

There was still a Temple tax in the New Testament period; Jesus used a coin taken from a fish to pay it (Mt.17:24–27).

Temple worship

The bread set out on the table (verse 33) *Shewbread,* or the 'bread of the presence' in the post-exile period was called the 'bread set out in rows'. It was also referred to as the 'bread of the face' because it was put before the face or presence of God (Ex.25:30; 35:13).

It involved twelve loaves or cakes of bread set in two rows. Alongside each row was placed frankincense as a memorial to the presence of the Lord. It was then set on fire as an offering to God (Lv.24:7). Afterwards Aaron and his sons (the priesthood) would eat their share of bread as holy people (Lv.24:9).

Casting lots (verse 34) Casting lots was a way of discerning the will of God (Lv.16:8; 1 Sa.14:42; 1 Ch.26:13,14; Ne.11:1). The soldiers cast lots for Jesus' clothes at the cross. It was not gambling but a method of discovering the divine will of God (Mt.27:35; Mk.15:24; Lk.23:34; Jn.19:24; compare with Ps.22:18).

The sacred lots were called *Urim* and *Thummim* (Ne.7:65; see the note on Ezra 2:63).

The wood offering (verse 35) Wood was used for the altar fire in order to burn the offerings (Lv.1:17; 6:12–13). But there is no information about whose responsibility it was to obtain the wood. It is typical of Nehemiah's concern with practicalities that he covers this detail.

Personnel

Aaronite priest (verse 38) Aaronite ancestry of the priesthood is only stressed in Ezra and Nehemiah (Ezr.7:1–5; Ne.12:47). Ezekiel refers to the priests as the 'sons of Zadok' (Ezk.40:46; 44:15; 48:11). His descendants were priests in the first temple.

The Aaronite priests were entitled to a tenth of the Levites' income (Nu.18:26–28). So there may be some implication that the priests should be present to check the Levites' income.

History

Marriage (verse 30) See the notes on Ezra 10:2, 10:11 and 10:13.

Nehemiah 11:1–19

Faith in the city

The nation could never be strong while the city was weak. There must be faith in the city in order to have faith in the nation.

The Temple was rebuilt, the walls of the city were restored and there was a revival of the covenant between God and his people. There was even good news for the poor. Things were looking good, there was just one problem. Nobody was queuing up to live in the city.

There were priests and Levites, as well as Temple staff, living in Jerusalem. Some of the leaders involved in the administration also lived there, but it was not what might be called a balanced community – socially and economically.

The action of the people brought a new perspective on tithing when they sought the will of God for one in ten from every pure Jewish family to move back into the city. It was fine rebuilding Jerusalem, but not much would be achieved unless the people of God were prepared to have enough faith in their city to live there. If it was taken over by Samaritans, Gentiles and other foreigners then who would be to blame when once again the Temple and the walls fell into disrepair. Whose fault would it be when Jerusalem could no longer be called the 'Holy City of God'?

God could not find ten righteous people in the city of Sodom, and gave this as his reason for destroying it (Gn.18:32). Ezekiel gives us a further insight into the destruction of Sodom when he states that it was destroyed because its people did not care for the poor and needy (Ezk.16:49).

Too often great cities have fallen into decay because the people of God have moved out to the comfortable suburbs. City churches have fallen into disrepair, been sold off to become temples of other faiths, warehouses, etc. Cities of the world have become the focus for all kinds of problems: poverty, crime, drugs, homelessness, godlessness, but rarely the glory of God.

The call of Nehemiah is still valid today, to have faith in the city is to do something about it. Where are the one in ten Christians today who are prepared to sell up and move back into the cities in order to restore the faith of the nation ? If we don't take our cities for God today there is no hope for the rest of the nation tomorrow!

Questions

1. How many of us live within walking distance of the place where we worship?

2. Are there enough Christians living close to each other in your community to make a difference?

3. What does it mean for the people of God to be salt and light in the nation (see Mt.5:13–16)?

Personnel

The leaders of the people (verse 1) Nehemiah 7:4–5 hints that because of the small population of the city some nobles were encouraged to move in. This verse appears to confirm that this was true. Earlier Nehemiah took the initiative, now it appears to be the people themselves, so things were improving.

It is unlikely that this meant all the leaders. It was probably those who were most involved in the decision-making processes of the nation on both the religious and secular levels. Jerusalem would be the administrative centre for the province under Persian rule as well as the focal point of worship because of the Temple.

The people commended (verse 2) More literally, 'the people gave their blessing'. This was something reserved for those who volunteered to live in the city rather than waiting to be told. The same word for 'volunteer' is used of military service (Jdg.5:2; Ps.110:3).

Judah and Benjamin (verses 4–9) A more comprehensive list of the inhabitants of Jerusalem is recorded in 1 Chronicles 9. Nehemiah records only the lay leadership of the tribes of Judah and Benjamin. There are more tribal sub-divisions given here than in Nehemiah 7.

It was only the tribes of Judah and Benjamin (with priests and Levites) that returned from exile (Ezra 1:5).

Brave men (verse 6) Brave men *(anashi chayil)* can also be translated 'men capable of bearing arms' or 'men of substance'. If it is read in context with 'brave warriors' *(gibbor chayil)* or 'men capable of bearing arms' (verse 14) it can be seen that a military emphasis is intended.

Haggedolim (verse 14) The name translates as 'the great (men) ones'. Was it a proper name or not? Some scholars think that it is the slip of a pen (a scribal error) for *haggadol* (high priest). Another alternative which is offered is that 'the great ones' were men of one of the leading families of the time. There is no definite answer to the question at this time.

The gatekeepers (verse 19) The two families Akkub and Talmon were Temple gatekeepers (see the note on Ezra 2:42) and not city gatekeepers (see the note on Ne.7:3).

Nehemiah 11:20–36

Town and country

It is important to recognize God's presence wherever we live, not just in special places, as well as our part in his plans.

Thirty-two towns, villages or farms are listed here as being at least partly occupied by Jewish people, in an area which was traditionally allocated to the tribes of Judah and Benjamin.

It would be perfectly natural for people returning from exile to want to return to their home towns, back to their roots where they felt they belonged. Belonging, however, has to be in the perspective of the wider community of the people of God: not just 'you in your small corner and I in mine'.

This passage not only names the towns, but also locates them in the perspective of the country. Each has its part to play and, therefore, is worthy of mention.

I feel certain that it was Nehemiah's concern that every devout Jew should feel involved in this time of restoration of Jerusalem. So it would be with this in mind that he looked to 'the rest of the people' (Ne.11:1) to send folk from their families to live in Jerusalem.

Pethaniah (verse 24) has another part to play in God's plans. He was the king's agent for the region and you can be sure that, as a practising Jew, he was also working for *the* King!

It is a firm reminder that God has a part for each one of us to play in his purposes, no matter how insignificant we may feel we are. It is important to know how God wants to use us where we live, but also to understand that we also belong to the worldwide family of God's people through our blood ties in Jesus Christ.

The great challenge is to be 'salt and light' (an influence for good; Mat.5:13–16) wherever we are, and to proclaim the good news of Jesus: the opportunity for forgiveness and a new beginning for all who want to be a part of his family.

Paul, the apostle, puts it clearly when he writes, 'in Christ we who are many form one body, and each member belongs to all the others' (Rom.12:5).

Sometimes we can feel isolated, but we are not. As Christians we are all a part of God's mighty army. When you feel you are struggling remember the words of a song by Ishmael, a Christian song-writer and singer, 'we may be weak as soldiers – but as an army we are strong', ('We are in God's Army' by Ian Smale, published by Thank You Music, 1987).

Questions

1. *How does my church relate to the worldwide church of Jesus Christ?*

2. *What did Jesus mean when he prayed, 'that all of them may be one, Father, just as you are in me and I am in you' (Jn.17:21)?*

3. *Are there ways in which I can be the King's agent where I live?*

Geography

The villages with their fields (verse 25) 'Fields' may also be translated 'farms'. Seventeen of them are mentioned in the land of Judah, fifteen in the land of Benjamin.

All the Judean towns and villages named in Nehemiah 11:25–36, with the exception of Dibon, Jeshua and Meconah, are also listed in Joshua 15:20–32. As a result some scholars think that Nehemiah has copied Levitical lists (Jos.21:8f; 1 Ch.4:23f). If this is true then why has he omitted some of the key places in the lists (Jos.18:11–28)?

Also, the land area covered by these towns and villages is a much larger area than might be expected during this period of Israel's history. For instance, the ones in the Negev must have been part of Geshem's territories (verse 35). The valley of Ono was part of a no-man's land at this time (see the note on Ne.6:2).

My own feeling is that rather than actual Jewish territories these were places with significant Jewish communities. As members of the Persian Empire they would be allowed to settle in any of the provinces and did so.

Rather than a copied list with some omissions it may be that this was a list of fortified towns and villages a bit like the more modern kibbutzim in Israel today. In the kibbutzim people live in a farming community surrounded by a perimeter fence guarded by members of the community. Another possibility is that it was a list of places which were not directly touched by the Babylonian conquest.

The settlements (verse 25) They all give the picture of ancestral territories (verse 20) extending from Beersheba in the south to the northern edge of the land of Judah (Jos.15:8), surrounding the Temple like the camp of Israel around the Tabernacle in the wilderness (Nu.2:1–2; see Map 4).

Ten settlements mentioned come within a twenty-mile radius of Beersheba which was under Edomite/Arab jurisdiction at this time.

Zorah to Azekah (verses 29–30) were in Shephelah, a lowland area running down to the flatlands of the coast.
Kiriath Arba (verse 25) was another name for Hebron (Jos.14:15) and was 25 miles south of Jerusalem.
Dibon (verse 25) is not the Dibon of Isaiah 15:9. Its location today is probably El Qebab, Debir (Jos..21:15) 22 miles east of Beersheba.
Jekabzeel (verse 25) or Kabzeel is thought to be either Tel Ira or Kh al-Ghara, the district capital and between 12 and 15 miles east of Beersheba (Jos.15:21).
Jeshua (verse 26) is probably Shema (Jos.15:26) modern day Tel

Jeshua 15 miles east of Beersheba.

Moladah (verse 26) today is Kheireibet el-Waten (Jos.15:26). It is located 2 miles east of Beersheba.

Beth-pelet (verse 26) is thought to be either Tell es-Saqati, or Tell el-Milh (Jos.15:27) about 6 miles north-east of Beersheba.

Hazar Shual (verse 27) meaning 'the Jackal's enclosure', is also mentioned in Joshua 15:28, Kh. Wa an today.

Beersheba (verse 27) is the ancient site of Tell es-Saba' (Jos.15:28) which is 2 miles east of the town known as Beersheba today.

Ziklag (verse 28) is probably Tell esh-Shari'ah which is 13 miles north-west of Beersheba (Jos.15:31).

Meconah (verse 28) is the only name which we can be certain is absent from the Joshua list. It may well be Madmannah, 10 miles north-east of Beersheba.

En-rimmon (verse 29) is the Pomegranate Spring of Joshua 15:32 and 19:7. It is around 9 miles north-east of Beersheba.

Zorah (verse 29) is now accepted as being Sariah (Jos.19:41), 17 miles west of Jerusalem. It was Samson's home town (Jdg.13:2).

Jarmuth (verse 29) is Kh. Yarmukin in the same area (Jos.15:35).

Zanoah (verse 30) is 3 miles south of Jerusalem (Jos.15:34).

Adullam (verse 30) referred to in Joshua 15:35 is 9 miles south of Jerusalem.

Lachish (verse 30) 20 miles south-west of Jerusalem (Jos.15:39) is now Tell el-Duweir. It was one of the major Jewish defences of the hill country.

Azekah (verse 30) 6 miles south-east of Lachish (Jos.15:35) is mentioned in the *Lachish Letters* (letters discovered at Lachish in 1935–38 dating from about 589 BC). Today the site is called Tell ez-Zakaiyeh.

Valley of Hinnom (verse 30) runs along the southern wall of the city of Jerusalem.

Geba, Bethel and Aija (verse 31) – Ai of Joshua fame (Jos.7:2) – were 6 to 11 miles north of Jerusalem.

Nob (verse 32) is Nebo (Ezr.2:29) and is a hill which overlooks Jerusalem from the north (Is.10:32).

Anathoth and Ananiah (verse 32) are also within 3 miles of Jerusalem. Ananiah is usually accepted as being Bethany, the home of Lazarus (Jn. 12:1).

Hazor (verse 33) is not the chariot city of Solomon in Naphtali, recently excavated by professor Yigael Yadin. It is Tel Asur or Baalnazur 15 miles north of Jerusalem (2 Sa.13:23).

Ramah (verse 33) or Ramleh (Ezr.2:26) is 5 miles north of Jerusalem.

Gittaim (verse 33), that is the two Gaths, is probably Tell Ras Abu Hamid near Ramah.

Hadid, Zeboim and Neballat (verse 34) **Lod, Ono, and the Valley of the Craftsmen** (verse 35) were all on the coastal plain around about 30 miles north-west of Jerusalem.

For **Lod** (verse 35) see the note on Nehemiah 6:2.

The Valley of the Craftsmen (verse 35) could be linked with Joppa. Joppa was the nearest port to Jerusalem for unloading timber from Lebanon (Ezra 3:7) so this could be an area well known at the time for its carpenters and timber craftsmen.

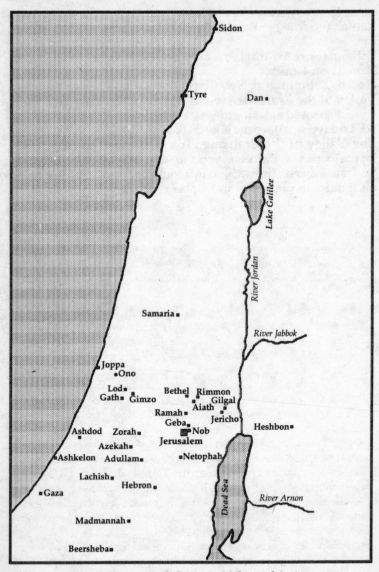

Map 4: Towns and Cities in Nehemiah's time

Nehemiah 12:1-26

God's worship leaders

The chief purpose of man (including woman) is to glorify God.

In this section Nehemiah records various lists detailing the names of the priests and heads of the priestly families and the leaders of the Levites.

The first list of priestly families is identified by its family heads and were those who had returned from exile in Babylon with Zerubbabel and Jeshua in 537 BC just after Cyrus' proclamation. It was always the priestly families who would lead the people of God into his presence in public worship.

Twenty-two names are listed here (verses 1–7) which have caused some discussion among scholars because normally twenty-four leaders were required to organize the Temple duties (1 Ch.24:1–8). Some scholars suggest this list is a faulty copy which has resulted in two names being omitted. Or it might be that because these were still early days in the restoration of Jerusalem, the priestly functions were not yet fully operational.

The second list of names is those of Levitical families at the time of the return from exile (verses 8,9). Although Ezra 2:4 records that seventy-four Levites returned to Jerusalem it only mentions the names of the two leaders, Jeshua and Kadmiel, plus the family name of Hodaviah, whereas Nehemiah records more details. The Levites were given the responsibility for leading thanksgiving and praise in the great celebration (verses 8,24) as well as other tasks such as gatekeepers and guarding the store-rooms of the Temple (verse 25).

The third list of names concerns the priests of the following generation, that of Jeshua's son Joiakim. This list, like the others, confirms the fact that the priestly families retained their ancestral names rather than change them every time a new leader was appointed.

In some translations the spelling of the names varies between the two lists which has led some scholars to believe that the second list was a later addition. However, it is much more likely that spelling changed with the generations, (as did the English language until dictionaries were invented) and that the second list was written by Nehemiah at the same time as the first. Further, it has been quite common in recent times for Jews moving from one country to another to modify their names in order to adapt to the new culture – for example Levi, Levine, Levinski.

The final list is the heads of the Levites in Eliashib's time (verses 22–26). The date would have been around 450 BC and onwards. Time was usually measured in terms of the lifespans of the high priests before there were kings in Israel. It appears that with the demise of the rule of kings, time was again measured in relation to priests and Levites.

The New Testament develops the concept of priesthood a stage further. It puts the emphasis on Jesus as the great high priest (Heb.4:14–16) and Peter writes of those who are disciples of Jesus as 'a royal priesthood, a holy nation' (1 Pet.2:5); out of interest, the Latin word for priest means 'bridge-maker'.

Today each one who answers the call to follow Jesus is called to the priesthood of all believers. Everyone who believes has a responsibility to regularly come before God in worship, thanksgiving and praise. No longer is it valid to believe there is some form of priesthood who will carry out these responsibilities on our behalf: it is our duty and should be our delight. We live in a world where everyone seems to be concerned with their *rights*, this is our *responsibility*. This is the new covenant.

Questions

1. Do you worship only when you feel like it? If so, do you only pay your taxes on the same basis?

2. Is Jesus the only go-between (bridge) necessary between you and the Heavenly Father?

3. What do you think the role of the priest is, as mentioned in I Peter 2:5?

Personalities

And Joiarib (verses 6, 19) Joiarib was an ancestor of the famous Jewish freedom-fighting family, the Maccabees, in the time of the Greek Empire (1 Maccabees 2:1 in the Apocrypha). The name also appears in the list of 1 Chronicles 24 as one of the priestly divisions. The NIV misses out the 'and' before Joiarib's name, but it is there in the Hebrew. It probably was there to indicate that the names which followed were taken from a second list.[31]

Sherebiah (verse 8) This name is also found in Nehemiah 8:7; 9:4 and 10:12.

Mattaniah (verse 8) and **Bakbukiah** (verse 9) also occur in Nehemiah 11:17 and 12:25.

Unni (verse 9) is a variation on the name Ananiah or Anaiah (compare 1 Ch.15:18 and 20 with Ne.8:4 and 3:23).

The family names of the Levites are also found in the list of King David's musicians in 1 Chronicles 25:4 with the same responsibilities.

Families of the high priests are next (verses 10–11). 1 Chronicles 6:3–15 gives the lineage of the high priests from Aaron to Jozadak. Jozadak was high priest at the time of the exile (Ezr.3:8; 5:2; 10:18; Hg.1:1; Zc.6:11).

Jeshua (verse 10) was Jozadak's son (Ezr.3:2) and was one of those who returned in 538 BC.

Joiakim (verse 10) was high priest in the period between the return of Jeshua and Zerubbabel and the return of Nehemiah.

Eliashib (verse 10) was high priest during Nehemiah's governorship (Ne.3:1, 20–21; 13:28).

Joiada (verse 10) was related to Sanballat (Ne.13:28).

Jonathan (verse 11) is sometimes thought to be the same person as Johanan because the historian Josephus[32] names him as the next high priest after Eliashib. This is not my view (see the note on Ezra 10:6) especially as Josephus is notorious for getting both his facts and dates confused.

Jaddua (verse 11) according to Josephus[33] was high priest at the time of Alexander the Great which would be about 332 BC. If he is correct then Jaddua must have been about 100 years of age by then. What is more reasonable is to assume that this was a family name and therefore there was more than one Jaddua who was high priest over the years.

Ezra (verse 13) is an alternative form of Azariah (see the notes on Ezr.7:1 and Ne.10:2).

Zechariah (verse 16) is the prophet Zechariah of the book of that name. He is a descendant of Iddo (see the note on Ezr.5:1).

Jedaiah (verses 19, 20) is a name which appears twice and would seem to confirm the idea that they were actually two different people.

Darius the Persian (verse 22) The question is, which Darius? Was it Darius the Great (522–486 BC), Darius II also called Nothus (423–405 BC) or Darius III also known as Codomannus (335–330 BC) and last ruler of the Persian Empire before the conquest of Alexander the Great?

The date which best fits the context is Darius II and this is supported by the Elephantine papyri which record that Johanan, Bagoli and Sanballat all held office during the reign of Darius II.[34]

Biblical terms

David the man of God (verse 24) This is a phrase which you would expect to be developed by the Levitical guilds of musicians referred to in this verse (see 1 Ch.16:4; 23:30; 25:1–8; 2 Ch.8:14; 29:25). David was well-known for his musical skills and so would be a popular figure with musicians. Moses was well-known for bringing the Law to God's people so Ezra, with his religious law training, gives Moses the same title: 'man of God' (Ezr.3:2).

Jeshua son of Kadmiel (verse 24)
Jeshua raises an interesting question. Why is he the only one mentioned here by both his name and family name? The idea has been put forward that this was 'a slip of the pen' or the handwriting (remember there were no printing presses) has been misread. The implication is that the Hebrew 'Jeshua Ben Kadmiel' should actually read 'Jeshua', 'Bani', 'Kadmiel' (compare Ne.9:4; 10:9–13; 12:8). Certainly the three names come together in a number of instances, and there is little difference between Ben and Bani in Hebrew.

The book of the annals (verse 23) *The book of chronicles* in some versions. It is not the biblical book of that name but a *lost book* of family trees and records which would have been kept in the Temple archives.

Nehemiah 12:27–30

Come on and celebrate!

Although the work was done by human hands it was God who made it possible – he should be given his rightful place, it is his party.

This passage takes us back into Nehemiah's diary for an account of what happened next: the dedication of the wall. It was not only temples which were singled out for celebrations. The completion of the wall was Nehemiah's greatest achievement and the climax of his governorship.

Worship leaders were brought in from the surrounding towns and villages including singers, choirs and musicians. This was going to be some celebration!

As with any great celebration there was plenty of planning to do if it was going to be done properly. Levites were sent out to the Jewish communities surrounding Jerusalem. It was going to be a holy day and a holiday so everyone and everything involved had to be purified. After all, this celebration was in God's honour. This was to be a time of thanksgiving to him as well as the dedication of all that had been achieved in his name.

Not many people would dream of inviting the Queen of England to a party without a good deal of time spent in thought, planning and preparation. Most folk would take a lot of time and trouble to ensure the place was clean and tidy. Personal appearance would be a priority as well. They would want everything to look its best and the aim would be to make a good impression with their 'VIP' visitor. If given the chance, they would almost certainly want to invite all their family, friends and neighbours.

Is that how we prepare for worship – the time when we come in a very special way into the presence of the King of kings?

Isaiah did not feel right in the presence of a holy God until he was clean right through (Is.6:6–8); then his heart's desire was to serve God in the very best way possible.

When the woman at the well met Jesus she simply had to invite everyone she knew to come and meet him (Jn.4:29). As a result many of them became believers and wanted Jesus to stay with them (Jn.4:39–40).

It does not matter where Christians meet to celebrate God's goodness; God should be given his rightful place.

The pattern that Nehemiah followed in preparing for worship was: preparation, purification and praise. His invitation was, 'come on and celebrate'.

Questions

1. *How do you prepare for coming into the presence of God in worship?*

2. *Is your experience of him so exciting that you want to invite everyone you know to come and join in thanksgiving with you?*

3. *Would your church dedicate a wall, a car or a 'fridge if they believed God had provided it for them?*

Temple worship

Harps and lyres (verse 27) Sometimes translated 'harps and zithers', they were both stringed instruments and both were made of cypress wood. The first was played by plucking it with the fingers, and the second by strumming it with a plectrum. The lyre was the first instrument to be mentioned in the Bible (Gn.4:21); it had about ten strings on it, as did the harp.

Geography

Netophathite villages (verse 28) These were villages surrounding Netophah (Ezr.2:22) which was near Bethlehem (Ne.7:26). It was also the home of 'David's heroes' – the warriors who gained fame fighting with him (2 Sa.23:28–29).
Beth Gilgal (verse 29) This is probably Gilgal (the name in Hebrew can mean 'the rolling stones'). It was between Jericho and the river Jordan and the centre of operations when Israel crossed into the promised land (Jos.4:19). It was under twenty miles from Jerusalem so it was not too far for the singers to travel.
Geba (verse 29) Geba is also mentioned in Ezra 2:26 and Nehemiah 11:31. It was one of the Levitical cities listed in Joshua (Jos.21:17) which was around eight miles north-east of Jerusalem. The modern town of Jeba is situated in the same place today.
Azmaveth (verse 29) Also mentioned in Ezra 2:24, it was five miles north of Jerusalem.

Biblical terms

Purified (verse 30) Before any time of significant worship there was always some form of ritual purification (compare Ezr.6:20). The exact form which the purification took is not referred to, but various laws and traditions allow us to make an educated guess.
  For those ministering at the dedication purification would almost certainly mean fasting, ritual washing and abstaining from sexual intercourse.

There were very clear links between ritual purification and dedication or consecration to God. Impurity could occur as a result of: food eaten; the touching of various forms of dead flesh; childbirth; skin infections; mildew on clothing; bodily discharges; unlawful sexual relationships; and even lawful ones at the wrong time! (For more details see Lv.11–19.) Any state of impurity would separate the believer from God.

Jesus takes this a stage further when he states that wrong relationships between believers will have the same effect (Mt.5:23–24).

Nehemiah 12:31–43

Feet were made for walking

A walk of witness, worship and praise lets everyone know of the presence and provision of God.

The procession of praise has something of the flavour of Joshua and the Israelites when they marched around the city of Jericho, but Joshua was outside the city – these people were on the walls!

The walls had been worked on, they had been watched over, now the people were worshipping God while standing on them.

The procession was in two parts, one setting off to the right, and the other to the left, in order to meet half-way round.

Apart from proclaiming the ability of the Living God to help his people achieve the seemingly impossible task, Nehemiah was also making a point to his enemies. Remember how the opposition had sneered at the Jewish attempts at repairing the walls, how they had said that even a fox was not safe walking on it (Ne.4:3)?

Now there were two processions going around it, each being led by one of the two key people, under God, who had made it possible: Ezra and Nehemiah! Ezra took the southbound group and Nehemiah the group heading north.

Each procession was led by a choir, followed by dignitaries in order of importance. There was enough room for people to walk three abreast along it.[35] It started from the valley gate (see the note on Ne.2:13, 15) with the two groups eventually joining up again at the Temple. The sacrifices that were then made followed the same pattern as when the altar and the Temple were dedicated (Ezr.3:3–5; 6:17).

The atmosphere was one of worship as not only the religious leaders but many families participated. As on each of the significant moments previously recorded in Ezra and Nehemiah, it was a cause for great joy: a joy so powerful that the noise of it was heard far away!

God had brought his people back to their land, the Temple had been rebuilt, and now Jerusalem had been restored. Something exciting had been happening to the people through these events. They too had experienced restoration. God's people had discovered deliverance, determination and dedication again in their efforts to restore the glory of Almighty God in the land.

Whenever there has been any significant movement of the Spirit of God there have been processions of his people proclaiming his glory.

In recent times Christians have initiated something called 'March for Jesus'. A relatively small number of folk in London, England wanted to proclaim the name of Jesus in their city so they had a march through the city centre. Since then the movement has grown. There have been marches across every major town and city in Britain, many of the cities of Europe and then spreading throughout the world.

The pattern has been similar to that of Nehemiah: processions led by worship groups; witnessing to the power and provision of God in their lives; demonstrating the power of the Almighty to overcome the opposition; and not forgetting a real sense of joy so that the impact of it is far and wide.

Public proclamation of the saving power of Jesus, sharing not only his love, but also his joy, is one of the essential ingredients of a living church, a church which is on the march.

Two New Testament quotes come to mind: 'Go into all the world and preach the good news to all creation' (Mk.16:15) and, 'with your feet fitted with the readiness that comes from the gospel of peace' (Eph.6:15). Feet were made for walking.

Questions

1. *Has God done something in your life that you want to shout about? If so, what?*

2. *Why do you think that Christians often appear to prefer staying in when Jesus said, Go out?*

3. *What do you think the other peoples of Nehemiah's time thought of his walk witness?*

Personnel

Two large choirs (verse 31) The word which the NIV translates as 'choir', in Hebrew means 'giving thanks' or 'thanksgiving'. If you spoke to someone in Hebrew today you would use the same word to say 'thank you'. So a choir is a group of people gathered together to give thanks.

There were two choirs, the northern and the southern groups.

The southbound choir (verses 31–37) is listed first, it has seven priests (verses 33–35) and the choirmaster is Zechariah (verse 35). There are eight musicians (verse 36) and the rest of the group comprises half the leaders of Judah (verse 32) including Ezra (verse 36).

The northbound choir (verses 38–43) is similar in composition. There are seven priests (verse 41), Jezrahiah is the choirmaster (verse 42) and it also has eight musicians (verse 42). Nehemiah is in this procession (verse 38) and the other half of the officials (verse 40).

Seven priests (verses 41–42) may have some significance because there were seven priests in the procession that brought the ark of the covenant into Jerusalem (1 Ch.15:24). The number seven also has significance in Hebrew as the number for God and perfection. Hence the mark of the beast in Revelation 13:18 is 666, always short of perfection and identified with the monster of chaos.

Eight musicians may have some connection with the fact that in Ezekiel's vision of the new Temple the priests made their offerings on the eighth day (Ezk.43:27). Other links include: eight were saved in the ark (Gn.17:12) on the eighth day after the birth of a Jewish boy he is circumcised (Lv.12:3); and Micah 5:5 links seven shepherds and eight princes. We can only guess at this time the significance, if any, of these numbers.

What the choir sang is not recorded but scholars have linked Psalm 147 with this occasion.[36]

Biblical terms

Rejoicing and joy (verse 43) The word 'joy' or 'rejoice' appears here five times (see notes on Ezr.3:12–13; 6:22; Ne.8:10; 8:12).

Could be heard far away (verse 43) In Ezra 3:13 the noise the people made at the foundation-laying ceremony could also be heard far away. The one big difference is that then it was hard to distinguish between the weeping and shouts of joy; there was no such difficulty here!

Nehemiah 12:44–47

Maintaining ministry

The labourer deserves reward for work done.

Part of the promises the people of God had made was to pay their share in maintaining the Temple and ministry (Ne.10). The priests, Levites, Temple gatekeepers and musicians all needed to live, so Nehemiah ensured that they were not taken for granted. He encouraged the people to give, but the Levites had the responsibility of 'taking the plate round'.

They went out to the surrounding towns and villages to take up collections to maintain the ministry of the Temple; it was not a freewill offering but an obligatory collection. The spirituality of Israel was at a high point at this time so the people gave gladly.

Something of the same feel existed in the New Testament Church. After Pentecost, when people were being added daily to the Church, there were no real money problems. They shared willingly what they had with those in need (Acts 4:32), with one or two notable exceptions (Acts 5:1–11).

Even when the church in Jerusalem experienced a time of famine Paul could write to other churches around the Roman Empire encouraging them to give their members to give generously. He encouraged them with the words, God loves a cheerful giver'

(2 Cor.9:7) and challenged the churches to out-give each other.

When people are blessed by God through his servants, it should be only natural (supernatural) to want to give to God and his work. Giving should be not just a duty, but a delight.

There are three kinds of giving: grudge-giving, nudge-giving and thanks-giving. The only one the Almighty really finds acceptable is thanksgiving.

Questions

1. *Could I survive if God gave me nine times as much as I give him and I had to live on it?*

2. *Do you think people of God should be paid, or should they earn their own keep?*

3. *Why do so many churches in Britain seem to have difficulties raising money for the upkeep of the buildings, and maintenance of ministry?*

History

First fruits (verse 44) Better translated 'the prime fruits' because the offering given to God was not necessarily the first to ripen but the best. The word 'first' comes from a Hebrew root word, *rosh*, meaning 'prime', 'chief' or 'head' indicating the very best of its kind. The same word is used in chapter  10:37 but chapter 13:31 uses a different word meaning 'the first fruit to ripen'.

Geography

From the fields around the towns (verse 44) Each town had the size of its contribution to the Temple assessed according to the amount of farmland it included.

233

Personalities

In the days of Zerubbabel and of Nehemiah (verse 47) refers to the Zerubbabel who was part of the first return and Nehemiah the cupbearer. Both were well known governors of the province but some years apart. This passage is easier to understand if it is read 'in the days of Zerubbabel and (the days) of Nehemiah'.

Although the remark is that the Temple contributions were made on a regular basis, the collection was not without its problems (Ne.13:10).

Nehemiah 13:1–3

Keep it clean

God's people are called to be in the world but not of the world.

Nehemiah kept his promise to the Persian king, Artaxerxes, and returned to the palace after the task of restoring the wall (and the people) had been completed.

There is an old saying, 'while the cat is away the mice will play', and that seemed to be exactly the situation in Judah after Nehemiah's return to Babylon. Now it was necessary, all over again, for the Jews to 'clean up their act' and separate themselves from the foreigners in the land. Those listed in the category 'All who were of foreign descent' (verse 3) could include not only Ammonites and Moabites, but any Jew who had non-Jewish ancestors, that is, mixed blood. We know that this restriction was not put fully into action, otherwise all of King David's descendants would have been excluded: his grandmother, Ruth, was a Moabite (Ru.1:4; compare Mt.1:5). My feeling is that it means immigrants who have no Jewish blood, rather than the other way round. As in chapter 9:2, there is no reference to separating from foreign wives, but the Jews were told to clean up their act.

The early Church used a ship as a symbol for the Church. It is a good way of understanding the nature and mission of the covenant people of God. We are called to weather out the storms of life, sailing wherever the wind of the Spirit takes us and with Jesus Christ as our anchor. A ship on the sea is safe as long as the water is outside the ship and not inside. Christians are safe while they remember to be in the world but not of the world.

Someone once made the observation, 'the Church is called to be in the world, but we must not allow the world to infect the church'. Our commitment is to do things God's way without compromise, and not allowing the pressure of the people to get in the way.

The trend of the world, like the story of Balaam, is to do what the majority want and think: go along with the crowd or risk persecution. But the outcome is still the same: God blesses those who are persecuted for his sake (Mt.5:11–12).

The call to the Church today is the same call given in the time of Nehemiah, keep it clean!

Questions

1. *What sort of pressures are there on Christians today to compromise their faith?*

2. *What would you say to someone who told you that Christians should not be so arrogant in insisting that Jesus Christ is the only way to heaven?*

3. *What is your church's view of what God says in his Word about homosexuality, abortion, and war?*

Times and seasons

On that day (verse 1) The phrase has already been used in chapter 12:44, although the NIV translates it there, 'at that time'. Both refer to time which is not specific and 'at that time' is probably the better translation in the context.

Geography

Ammonite or Moabite (verse 1) Both nations were descendants of Lot through an incestuous encounter with his daughters (Gn.19:33–38) which is probably why they are linked together on the issue of unacceptable relationships, despite the fact that the encounter with Balaam only involved the Moabites (Nu.22–25), although tradition holds that Baalam was an Ammonite.

Personalities

Balaam (verse 2) Balaam was a pagan seer and sorcerer who was hired by the king of Moab to curse Israel, but every time he cursed them the curse was turned into a blessing (Nu.23:11; 24:1, 10).

Biblical terms

The book of Moses (verses 1–2) This is a quotation from Deuteronomy 23:3–5 (see the note on Ezr.6:18).

237

Nehemiah 13:4–9

Cleansing the Temple

To make room for God means getting rid of the rubbish.

Nehemiah obtained permission from Artaxerxes to pay a return visit to Jerusalem (verse 6) and as he does so the account returns to the first person, indicating that he is again drawing from his diary.

How easily the people had settled down to a comfortable compromise after Nehemiah's departure. His arch-enemy Tobiah (an Ammonite!) had taken up lodgings in the Temple (verses 4–5). The fact that he had married into one of the priestly families, and his son into another, helped him to move in. Many of the Jewish leaders had made an oath of allegiance to him (see the note on Ne.6:18–19). 'A room in the courts' (verse 7) would be a room of some size opening up into the courtyard of the Temple. The word which is translated 'a room' suggests not only a store-room but also living accommodation (1 Ch.9:26; 2 Ch.31:11; Ezra 8:29; Ne.10:38–40).

The presence of a non-Jew here would require purification of the whole area from ritual uncleanness (see the note on Ne.12:30).

On his return Nehemiah had no hesitation, he threw Tobiah out with all his belongings. Then he set about having the Temple rooms purified. What must have really annoyed him was the fact that

Tobiah had taken over rooms set aside for the offerings for the Temple staff and the incense for God.

This event links with the time when Jesus entered the Temple and threw out the money-changers accusing them of making his father's house a den of robbers instead of a house of prayer (Mt.21:13; Mk.11:17; Lk.19:46; he was quoting from Is.56:7 and Je.7:11).

It is so easy for things to creep into the life of the church through wrong relationships and unholy alliances. Once things, or people which are nothing to do with God move into the Body of Christ it does not take long for the rot to set in. As mentioned it is like the bad apple – it only takes one to gradually affect and infect all the rest.

The only way out is to 'take the bull by the horns', and get rid of them completely. Holiness is not negotiable; cleanse the temple!

Questions

1. *What connection is there between a jolly fat man with reindeer and the birth of Jesus?*

2. *Does your church think it is acceptable to God to hold an act of worship with people of other faiths, each praying to their own deity?*

3. *Can you think of examples of people or things which have moved in and taken over the place of God in your life?*

Times and seasons

32nd year of Artaxerxes (verse 6) That is, 433 BC, but we do not know the exact date of Nehemiah's return visit. Inasmuch as he came with Artaxerxes permission it has to be before the king's death in 423 BC.

Personalities

Eliashib This was not Eliashib the high priest of 3:1,20–21; 12:10,22, and 13:28. This Eliashib is not referred to as high priest; his responsibility was to look after the Temple rooms, the equivalent of a dean. He certainly would gain from letting out the rooms. The fact that Eliashib the high priest was related to Sanballat, another of Nehemiah's foes (13:28) probably helped set a precedent.

A similar incident happened in Egypt when King Cambyses cleansed the temple of the god Neith, having thrown out all foreigners.[37]

History

Frankincense (verse 5) Frankincense is a white resin taken from the Boswellia tree. It is one of the ingredients of incense (Ex.30:34). It was expensive and was used as an offering to God. Only the priests were allowed to use it and there were clear instructions on how it should be used (Lv.16:12). It came to be used as a symbol of prayer (Ps.141:2) and was one of the gifts given to Jesus by the astrologers or Magi (Mt.2:11).

Nehemiah 13:10–14

Robbing God

Neglecting the things of God will always lead to problems.

What a change from chapter 12:44–47 when the people were so willing to give. Now they have moved from thanks-giving to grudge-giving. The financial crisis at the Temple was so great that many of the Temple staff have been forced to go home in order to have enough to eat (verse 11).

It was necessary for Nehemiah to put God's house in order; he was not a priest but it looks as though the high priest was not doing his job properly because of self-interest. First Nehemiah got the Temple staff back and then he set up a finance committee.

The people he chose were appointed not for their skills, but their trustworthiness. Too often people are appointed for their ability rather than their spirituality, but Nehemiah had played before!

Almost the last words of the Old Testament are on the same topic – robbing God. The plea is,'Bring the whole tithe into the store-house, that there may be food in my house' (Mal.3:10). The promise which follows is that if the people will respond, God will bring them a blessing so great they will not be able to contain it (Mal.3:11). Presumably they ignored the call because soon after Alexander the Great came, took over the land and desecrated the Temple.

Not much has changed; there are still churches which struggle to survive financially because they give God the left-overs instead of the best, while others have rediscovered that what Malachi said is really true and their churches grow.

I remember someone once saying to me, 'You can never out-bless God, but it is great fun trying'. The message is plain, give to God and he will give to you, rob God and you will deprive yourself.

Questions

1. Which do you think comes first, financial problems or spiritual lethargy? Why?

2. If you were appointing a treasurer, musician or secretary for your church what qualities would you look for?

3. Why do you think some Christians begrudge giving to God's work when He even gave his only son for us?

Biblical terms

Remember (verse 14) The same word is used four times in this chapter (verses 14,22,29,31). It has only been used on five other occasions in the whole of Nehemiah (Ne.1:8; 4:14; 5:19; 6:14; 9:17).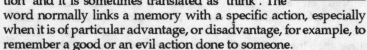

It means 'to call to memory', 'to record' or 'to mention' and it is sometimes translated as 'think'. The word normally links a memory with a specific action, especially when it is of particular advantage, or disadvantage, for example, to remember a good or an evil action done to someone.

Each reference here is in the form of a short prayer by Nehemiah, asking God to keep account of his good deeds (compare also Is.65:6; Dn.7:10; Rev.20:12).

The first part of the book of Nehemiah is significant for recording the number of times he prayed: however, no more personal prayers were recorded from chapter 6:14 until verse 14 in this chapter.

History

Portions assigned to Levites (verse 10) These were the tithes mentioned in chapter 10:37 which the people had promised to give. It may be that the Levites had not gone and collected them as was expected (12:44). It is also interesting that although technically Levites did not own land (Dt.14:29; 18:1; Nu.18:20–24) other than grazing land around their towns, these did (verse 10). So the ownership of land may have led to a conflict of interests for the Levites.

Nehemiah 13:15–22

Rest versus riches

However busy and demanding life is there should always be time for God and time for relaxation.

The first promise made is the hardest to break; after that it gets easier. First compromising with unbelievers, then giving God the left-overs and now riches come before rest and reflection. One by one the Jews broke the promises they had made so enthusiastically some time before (Ne.10:31).

The Law as given by Moses specifically stated that the Sabbath was to be a day of rest (Ex.20:8–11), even the animals are given a break (Ex.23:12). So making wine, loading grain and using donkeys was very much against the Law, let alone the covenant of chapter 10.

'My own men' (verse 19) suggests that Nehemiah evidently did not trust the local inhabitants to keep the gates closed (see the note on Ne.4:16). 'Night by the wall' (verse 21) refers to a method employed by tradespeople hoping to get to the head of the queue for when business began (rather as people nowadays queue up the night before the Harrods' sale begins). There was also the added possibility of doing some illegal trading with the guards or townspeople via baskets which they hung over the wall during the night.

Unbelievers put temptation in the way when they came to trade on the Sabbath. So much so that Nehemiah had to order the city gates to be closed just before the Sabbath began at sundown and not to be opened until the end of the Sabbath at sundown the following day.

How often throughout history the desire for power and wealth have overcome principles. It began in the garden of Eden (Gn.3:5), it prevented the rich young man following Jesus (Mt.19:16–24) and it caused the downfall of Ananias and Sapphira (Acts 5:1–10).

The church at the time of the Reformation was split because of a monk called Martin Luther. He took on the role of Nehemiah and challenged the Church over their corruption and accumulation of wealth instead of practising what they preached.

William Wilberforce had a struggle on his hands when he fought to abolish the slave trade because although many of the slave-owners were church-attending people, they were not willing to sacrifice wealth for the sake of freedom for their slaves.

Lord Shaftesbury experienced similar problems when he fought for better working conditions in the factories and the mines. Too many mine and mill owners were church-going folk who would lose money from the reforms.

Today it is Sunday which Christians observe as a special day of rest, relaxation and reflection. The Jewish rest day, Saturday, changed to the Christian rest day, Sunday, to remind believers that Jesus rose from the grave on Easter Sunday.

Wealth and power still get in the way of God's people. Sunday trading has meant even Christian-based companies cashing in through fear of losing out financially if they stick to their principles. People fear losing their jobs if they don't work on Sundays.

Some people have to work, such as doctors, police and preachers, but it is the motivation that is in question. Is it necessary or just financially beneficial?

God worked on creation for six days and rested on the seventh (Gn.2:3); we are made in his image and called to live his way. Jesus summed it up when he said, 'You cannot serve both God and Money' (Mt.6:24; Lk.16:13).

Apparently the French agnostic, Voltaire, said, 'If you want to kill Christianity you must abolish Sunday'. It is rest versus riches and we have to choose.

Questions

1. *Do you have a regular day off to relax and also spend time with God?*
2. *What would your church say if you had a normal Monday to Saturday job but your boss wanted you to work Sundays and you asked their advice?*

3. *Your family are not Christians but you live with them – they are using electricity illegally. What would you do?*

Biblical terms

I rebuked the nobles (verse 17) Nehemiah, as governor, was responsible for law and order. First he had tackled the priests; now he takes on the heads of the leading families in Jerusalem.

In telling them off he clearly states that Sabbath breaking was a direct cause of the Jews' subjection to foreign powers. A similar line was taken by Ezekiel and Jeremiah (Ezk.20:13; Jer.17:19–27).

Amos, a few centuries before, had prophesied that the wealthy rulers would be anxious about the Sabbath interfering with money-making (Amos 8:5).

Geography

Tyre (verse 16) See the note on Ezra 3:7.

Nehemiah 13:23–31

Drawing the Line

Non-believers usually cause their partners to move away from God.

'The language of Ashdod' (verse 24) was, like the Ammonite language, very similar to Aramaic (see previous notes on Aramaic), unlike the Moabite language that was very similar to Hebrew. Many Jews would have spoken Aramaic, probably a slightly different dialect, but Hebrew was and is the language of Jewish worship for the orthodox Jew.

Language is an important aspect of national identity, it was no different for the Jews then than it is for, say, the Welsh today.

On the surface the main issue is mixed marriages, but the underlying issue was the danger of losing national identity. This is why Nehemiah's complaint is that half the children of mixed marriages did not know how to speak the language of the Jews.

This would be a particularly sensitive problem with so many Jews living in other lands, and the dangers of assimilation (2 Ki.18:26,28; 2 Ch.32:8; Is.36:11).

So from Nehemiah's perspective it was about the survival of God's covenant people. There is sometimes a fine line between racial cleansing of the kind that Adolf Hitler would impose on the Jews many years later, and maintaining a national identity.

The same kind of situation arose in the New Testament Church when non-Jews at Antioch became followers of Jesus. Gentile believers were not willing to follow Jewish practices, but James ruled they could be part of the Church.

The dilemma was, should the Jewish Christians give up their national identity by forsaking the basic principles of their way of life such as kosher food laws, or circumcision (Acts 15:1–29)?

A similar issue arose out of Christians marrying non-Christians. Paul advised against it for the same reason as Nehemiah (2 Cor.6:14).

Christians marrying non-believers today still bring with them a number of problems. There will be conflicts of interest and probably beliefs. It is quite common for the unbelieving partner to pull the Christian away from faith and fellowship. When children are born whose way and example will they follow?

The only way to avoid this sort of conflict is to stay away from partnerships which lead to this sort of temptation.

Paul's comment on this subject is powerful, '...what fellowship can light have with darkness?...What does a believer have in common with an unbeliever?' (2 Cor.6:14,15).

Put another way, can oil and water mix?

Questions

1. Do you think Christians find it easier to be a Christian when they are with other Christians, or when they are with non-believers?

2. If someone in the family laughs at you because of your beliefs how do you react?

3. If you are married to a non-Christian and they say, if you really love me don't go to church, what would you say?

Biblical terms

Tore out their hair (verse 25) Hair pulling was a common practice of Old Testament times (Is.50:6) which suggests that beard plucking was a form of punishment and 2 Samuel 10:4–5 suggests that a man who had forcibly had his beard removed was the subject of humiliation, (see also the comments on Ezr.9:1–7).

Solomon's sin (verse 26) Solomon made treaties with other nations in order to improve trade and maintain peace in the land. In order to achieve this he entered into a number of marriages with daughters of nobles of those lands. When they came to Jerusalem they brought images of their gods with them and the tension began (1 Ki.3:12; 1 Ki.11:1–6).

Personalities

Eliashib and Sanballat (verse 28) Blood ties with the priesthood led to the same sort of difficulties for Eliashib as it did for Solomon (Lv.21:14 expressly forbids the high priest to marry a foreigner). So it should have come as no great surprise to him when Nehemiah threw Joiada, his son, out. Especially as
Sanballat was one of the main people to oppose Nehemiah in his efforts to rebuild the walls of Jerusalem (see the note on Ne.2:10).

Bibliographical References

1. Winton Thomas, *Documents from Old Testament Times* (Harper and Row, 1961) pp. 84–86.

2. S. Baron, *A Social and Religious History of the Jews* (Columbia University Press, 1952) p. 162.

3. J. Finegan, *Handbook of Biblical Chronology* (Princeton University Press, 1964) pp. 212–3.

4. Herodotus, *History* 1.98 (Everyman, 1992 edition) p. 56.

5. J. Stafford Wright, *The Date of Ezra's Coming to Jerusalem* (Tyndale, 1947) p. 26.

6. F. Vallat, 'L'Inscription Cuneiform Trilingue (D.Sab)' *Journal Asiatique* 260, (1972) p. 249.

7. *The Babylonian Talmud* (TB Sanhedrin 936).

8. F.C. Fensham, *The Books of Ezra and Nehemiah* (Wm. B. Eerdman's Publishing Co., 1982) p. 150.

9. Herodotus, *History* 3:34 (Everyman, 1992 edition) p. 233.

10. Xenophon, *Cyropaedia* 1.3, 8–9, 11 Quoted in J. Carl Laney, *Ezra–Nehemiah* (Chicago, Moody Press, 1982) p. 76.

11. Ernst Weidner, 'Hof und Halrems Erlasse', *Archiv für Orientforschung* Vol. 17 (1954–55) p. 11.

12. J.B. Pritchard (ed.), *Ancient Near Eastern Texts* (Princeton University Press, 1958) p. 492.

13. *Ibid.*, p. 492.

14. Josephus, *The Antiquities* 12:160–236, translated by William Whiston (London, Shapiro Valentine & Co., 1960) pp. 338–9.

15. Kathleen M. Kenyon, *Digging Up Jerusalem* (Book Club Associates, 1975) p. 185.

16. *Ibid.*, p. 182.

17. F.M. Cross, 'Geshem the Arab, Enemy of Nehemiah', *Biblical Archaeologist* 18 (1955) p. 46–47.

18. Josephus, *The Jewish War* 5.5.8 translated by G.A. Williamson (Middlesex, Penguin Classics, 1978) p. 75.

19. Kathleen M. Kenyon, *Digging up Jerusalem* (Book Club Associates, 1975) p. 83.

20. Kathleen M. Kenyon, *Jerusalem: Excavating 300 Years of History* (London, Ernest Benn Ltd., 1967) p. 111.

21. Josephus, *The Antiquities* 11.5.8 translated by William Whiston (London, Shapiro Valentine & Co., 1960) p. 313.

22. H. Koch, 'Steuern in der achamenidischen Persis?'*Zeitschrift für Assyriologieun Verderasiatische Archaeologie*, Vol. 70 (1981) pp. 105–37.

23. R.P. Maloney, 'Usury and Restrictions on Interest-Taking in the Ancient Near East', *Catholic Biblical Quarterly 36* (1974) pp. 1–20.

24. N. Avigad, 'Bullae and Seals from a Post-exilic Judean Archive', *Quedeh: Monographs of the Institute of Archaeology 4* (Jerusalem Hebrew University, 1976) pp. 1–20.

25. Kathleen Kenyon, *Digging Up Jerusalem* (Book Club Associates, 1975) p. 110.

26. Josephus, *The Antiquities* 11:179 translated by William Whiston (London, Shapiro Valentine & Co., 1960) p. 314.

27. R.A. Parker and W. Dubberstein, *Babylonian Chronology 626 BC-AD 75* (Providence, R.I., Brown University Press, 1956) – a monograph.

28. Warren W. Wiersbe, *Be Determined* (Scripture Press, 1992) p. 101.

29. Cyrus Gordon, *The Ugaritic Textbook 3* (Rome, Pontifical Biblical Institute, 1967) p. 381.

30. D.J. Clines, *Ezra, Nehemiah, Esther* (Marshall, Morgan & Scott Ltd.,1984) p. 205.

31. L.H. Brockington, *Ezra, Nehemiah and Esther* (London, N.C.B. Nelson, 1969) p. 155.

32. Josephus, *The Antiquities* 11.7.1 translated by William Whiston (London, Shapiro Valentine & Co., 1960) p. 322.

33. *Ibid.*, 11.8.4, p. 324.

34. F.M. Cross, 'The Discovery of the Samaria Papyri', *The Biblical Archaeologist* 26 (1963) pp. 110–121.
    F.M. Cross, 'Aspects of Samaritan and Jewish History in Late Persian and Hellenistic Times', *Harvard Review* 59 (1966) pp. 201–211.

35. Kathleen M. Kenyon, *Jerusalem* (London, Thames and Hudson, 1967) p. 115.

36. L.H. Brockington, *Ezra, Nehemiah and Ezra* (London, N.C.B. Nelson, 1969) p. 160.

37. Edwin M. Yamauchi, *Persia and the Bible* (Grand Rapids, Baker Book House, 1990) p. 106.

For further reading

P.R. Ackroyd, *Chronicles, Ezra, Nehemiah* (London, SCM, 1973).

Joseph Blenkinsop, *Ezra–Nehemiah* (London, SCM, 1989).

L.H. Brockington, *Ezra, Nehemiah and Esther* (London, NCB Nelson, 1969).

D.J.A. Clines, *Ezra, Nehemiah, Esther* (London, Marshall Morgan and Scott Ltd., 1984).

F.Charles Fensham, *The Books of Ezra, Nehemiah and Esther* (Grand Rapids, Eedrmans, 1991).

Derek Kidner, *Ezra and Nehemiah* (Leicester, IVP, 1979).

J. Carl Laney, *Ezra–Nehemiah* (Chicago, Moody Press, 1982).

Warren W. Wiersbe, *Be Determined* (Amersham on-the-Hill, Scripture Press, 1992).

H.G.M. Williams, *Ezra, Nehemiah* (Waco, Texas, Word Books, 1985).

Edwin Yamauchi, *Ezra, Nehemiah* (Grand Rapids, Regency Reference Library, Zondervan, 1988).

Edwin Yamauchi, *Persia and the Bible* (Grand Rapids, Baker Book House, 1990).